MW01671126

Unblock Writer's Block

How to face it, deal with it and overcome it

With over 70 writing exercises to get you started and keep you writing

Paul Lima

Published by
PAUL LIMA PRESENTS
www.paullima.com/books

Unblock Writer's Block
Copyright © 2013 by Paul Lima

Cover design and book layout by Paul Lima

Published by Paul Lima Presents
www.paullima.com

Manufactured in the U.S.A.
Published in Canada

All rights reserved. No part of this publication may be reproduced, stored in or introduced into a retrieval system, or transmitted in any form or by any means (electronic, mechanical, photocopying, recording or otherwise), without the prior written permission of both the copyright owner(s) and the above publisher of the book.

First Edition

Unblock Writer's Block
Lima, Paul

ISBN 978-0-9878711-9-0

This book is dedicated to those who overcome personal obstacles and work to nurture the writer within.

Introduction

There is no such thing as writer's block. How do I know? I know that there is no such thing as writer's block because I have a dog.

If you are feeling a tad quizzical right now, please stick with me.

As a writer, I live a sedentary life. I don't jog, lift weights or workout. Basically, I don't exercise. I do try to walk thirty minutes a day. Notice the word *try*. I am a fair weather walker. I walk when the weather is pleasant, not when it rains, sleets, hails or snows, or when it's too hot or too cold. If the weather is not fair, I have what might be described as walker's block.

Then my wife got a dog, a Giant Schnauzer named Kohl. We don't have a fenced in backyard and Kohl has to be walked twice a day. My wife walks him in the morning; I walk him in the afternoon. No matter the weather, I've walked my dog every afternoon for the last twelve years. In short, we have a dog and I no longer have walker's block.

The same principle applies to writer's block. You might think you have writer's block. What you lack is the writer's equivalent of a dog.

I am not playing down what one feels when one wants to write and can't write. In addition, I am not dismissing severe bouts of depression or anxiety that may inflict some writers (or anyone pursuing any art, craft or profession). But in the vast majority of cases, most of us who want to write are able to write—if we have a dog, or the writer's equivalent. This book is filled with dogs—writing exercises that will get you started and keep you writing.

With that in mind, welcome to *Unblock Writer's Block*. I hope the book helps you kick-start your writing and overcome whatever it is that may be keeping you feeling blocked.

Thanks to Heather Wright (http://wrightwriter.com), freelance writer and author of the book *Writing Fiction: A Hands-On Guide for Teens* for proofreading this book. She did an excellent job. Any typos you may see are all mine, made after the fact!

Paul Lima
www.paullima.com

Contents

1 / Yes, You Can Write

As mentioned in the introduction, I feel that there is no such thing as writer's block.

What an audacious thought. At least that is what you might be thinking if you are suffering from writer's block. And you may be, even if I think it does not exist.

The definition of writer's block is, simply put, "An inability to write." I am suggesting that anyone who knows how to write, and is physically able to do so, can write. In other words, does not have "an inability to write." But if you are not writing, or are having difficulty writing, then you feel blocked, no matter what I think. If you feel blocked, then this book should help you beat back whatever is blocking you, get you writing and keep you writing.

Most people who have writer's block have a reason (the equivalent of rain, sleet, hail or snow) to stop writing or lack a reason (a dog equivalent) to start writing. They may not like what they are producing or feel their writing is crap (more on that later), and stop, or they may lack ideas or not know where to go next with a story, and give up.

You may have stopped writing, but you are not blocked. Given a pen and paper, you can write. You may not have anything to focus your writing on, but you can write. You may not like what you write, but you can write. You may feel grumpy and petulant about writing, but you can write.

Yes, getting there might take more time than you'd like, and it might feel like a difficult chore. But then if it were easy, what fun would that be?

I am not saying you have to suffer for art. I am saying that sometimes writing feels like work. Because it is work. Also, I am not saying that writing is easy or that you will always be able to write what you think you want to write or that you will never struggle with writing or will not stop writing when you'd rather be writing. (In fact, it might not hurt you to stop writing occasionally to recharge your batteries, but a bit more on that later.)

So what am I saying? I am saying if you can write, then you don't have writer's block.

"But I have a mental block," you protest.

That does not mean you have an inability to write. You might not write your best stuff. You might even write gibberish or codswallop. But you can move beyond what feels like a block or an inability to write, and write.

So what if your writing is not perfect? Fact is, what most of us write, especially draft one or two or three or four—you get the picture—is, well, crap. Or as Ernest Hemmingway said, "The first draft of anything is shit."

That is part of writing, so you don't have writer's block if your writing isn't as good as you want it to be or if it is not flowing smoothly and eloquently. Smooth and eloquent writing is as much a part of the editing process as it is of the writing process. And if you stop writing because your first drafts are not perfect, you inflict writer's block upon yourself.

Again, I would never deny that some writers who want to write don't write. And I know writers who have indeed stopped writing. But I know many people who don't do a lot of things, or have stopped doing things they liked doing. When it comes to writing (or pretty much any other activity you are able to do), you only lose the ability to produce new work (or engage in the activity), if you stop. That doesn't mean you have lost the ability. It means you've stopped.

As someone who has been writing his own stuff for over 40 years, has been paid to write stuff for over 35 years, and has taught writing for over 25 years, I know that it can take work to start writing, to restart writing and to keep on writing.

Are you willing to do the work required to break through the block? That is the question.

This book is full of work you can do to start writing, but only you can choose to do the work.

And if that sounds a bit daunting, feel free to rephrase the above, two sentences: *This book is full of play you can do to start writing, but only you can choose to play.*

Play. Doesn't that feel better? Because that is what we are going to do here to help you overcome writer's block. We are going to play—play with words, situations, characters and stories—and make writing fun.

But allow me to digress for a moment and differentiate between writer's block and writer's procrastination.

Writers are famous for procrastinating. Or as the saying goes, "I've never met a deadline I couldn't ignore." Give writers deadlines, and watch them post thoughts on Facebook or Twitter, surf the web, update iPod playlists, check repeatedly for email, even check repeatedly for snail mail.

The writers may say they are blocked. They are not. They are procrastinating. Why? It might take a Dr. Phil or a therapist to answer that simple question. But if you have something to write about and you are frittering away your time, you are procrastinating, not blocked.

Just so you know, though, sometimes a bit of procrastination can be what you have to do to distract your conscious mind from the task at hand so your unconscious mind can process the work you have to do before you plunge in and start to write. So allow yourself a little procrastination time.

Having said that, sometimes you have deadlines to meet. Deadlines can be motivating, especially if missing one means you won't get paid for an article or won't receive an advance for a book. But if you have problems meeting deadlines, then you might be able to apply some of the writing exercises in this book (especially freefall and clustering) to do the work you have to do when a deadline is looming. There will be a bit more on this later.

Many writers, however, often work on projects—a novel, autobiography or work of non-fiction, for instance—that has not been sold to a publisher. Such writers lack deadlines. Where is the deadline motivation supposed to come from? In other words, you have to be self-motivated when you don't have a deadline. It can take a fair degree of self-discipline to motivate yourself. Look at all the published books out there that started as figments of the imaginations of writers who had no deadlines. It can be done.

Without a deadline, you may find yourself feeling blocked when you are, in fact, procrastinating. With that in mind, we'll also look at how you can impose deadlines on yourself to help you combat the lack of motivation and the procrastination that might accompany the lack of a deadline. For now, though, let us not confuse writer's procrastination, something a self-imposed kick in the butt or the fear of losing a pay check can cure, with writer's block.

Questions blocked writers should ask

Here are two questions writers who feel blocked should ask:

- Am I willing to produce work that does not meet my standards to get to the work that does?
- Am I willing to write, even though I don't know what I want to write about, to get to the work I want to write about?

If you've answered "no" to those two questions, you are not blocked. You have effectively decided to not do the work that is often required to write. And if you've answered "yes" to those questions, you may soon find yourself on a writing roll … but we are getting ahead of ourselves here, aren't we, talking about a writing roll when you believe moving forward at all is impossible.

If you feel as if you are stuck in a prisoner's block, and want out, then consider this book a set of tools baked in a cake and delivered to your cell. They will help you break out of the block, so you will be free to write again.

If you use the tools in this book and put pen to paper or fingers to keyboard, letters will appear. And some of those letters will form words. And some of those words will form sentences. And some of those sentences will form paragraphs. And so on and so on ...

And here you thought you were blocked.

So get ready to buckle down and write, no matter how you are feeling. And in many ways, that is the key—to write no matter how you are feeling. If you want to feel sorry for yourself, feel free. But buckle down. If you want to feel put upon or petulant, feel free. But buckle down. Because the problem, as you have defined it, is that you are blocked. And the solution, as I am defining it, is to write.

In other words, this book is not about feeling good. So feel whatever you are feeling, buckle down—and write!

2 / Why Writing Exercises?

Why is this book filled with writing exercises? You want to write and here I am suggesting that you do writing exercises. Is there a purpose to writing exercises?

Answer me this: Is there a purpose to gesture sketching that artists do, to voice exercises that singers do, to stretching that runners do, to rehearsing that actors do, to scales that pianists practise repeatedly? The answer is self-evident. This warming up—exercising, rehearsing and practising—helps the artist, singer, runner, actor, pianist do what they want to do.

Too often writers just want to write what they want to write. They want to sit down and, presto, produce the work. But they struggle with producing what they want to write, get frustrated and stop. Or they don't know exactly what it is they want to write, so they don't even start.

Writing exercises, on the other hand, are how writers warm up, practice and rehearse. They are how you get in shape. They are what you write for the sake of writing—in a no-pressure, not-for-publication situation. They are how you discover, or rediscover, the joy of writing. They are how you discover that you are able to write, that you don't have writer's block.

Or, to put it another way, try to leap off the couch and run a marathon without years of exercising and very specific training leading up to the marathon. Talk about out of breath and major cramps.

So why do so many of us insist on writing without exercising and getting into shape?

And, to continue our metaphor, let's say you actually run a marathon. Now do nothing for several months, other than eat all the pizza you want and drink all the beer your heart desires. Then try to leap off the couch and run another one. Talk about a recipe for failure.

So why does it surprise many writers that, after completing their first magnum opus and taking time off, they can't simply knock off their second one at the moment they choose? Why do they think they can ignore the need to exercise and get back into shape?

So that is what we are going to do here, exercise our writing muscles—muscles that may have been ignored, may have atrophied or may just need a little toning to get us back into writing shape.

And while you are working on the exercises here, keep this in mind: Even when you are writing without someone like me saying, "Here's what I suggest you do," you are seldom writing exactly what you want to write the way you want to write it. First, you finish the first draft of your short story, novel, poem, speech, report or pretty much any other document. Then you read it over and think, what a load of … and give up.

But that's where the magic begins. Once you have a first draft, you have something to work with, to convert from whatever it is to whatever you want it to be. Give up before you have completed that first draft and you have, well, given up. And hey, if that's what you want to do, nothing wrong with that—if you really want to do give up. Just recognize, please, that it is your decision. Like when I quit playing the guitar, *because it was too hard*. I regret it still, but I have to be a grown-up and acknowledge this: The guitar did not quit on me. I quit the guitar. I was not willing to do the work required to learn how to play as well as I imagined myself playing it.

Give up after you have completed that first draft, because your work is not as good as you want it to be, and you have, well, given up. It takes work to polish that first draft into something you want to show people. And then, once you get some feedback, it takes work to polish it again. And again. And yes, sometimes even again, and again.

"Is it ever easy?" you may ask.

When you are on a writing roll (and you may have experienced that), it can sure feel easy. But that does not mean it always will be, has to be or should be easy. And yes, on rare occasion, a passage will spring full born from your fingers, like the goddess Athena, the favourite daughter of Zeus, who sprung fully armed from her father's forehead. (But what a headache Zeus had afterwards, I tell you!) Such occasions, though, are rare, when the planets and stars align and strange cosmic forces take over your psyche and you write, almost unconsciously, on autopilot.

Find me a writer who writes like that at all times, and you will also be able to find me Big Foot, Yeti and the Loch Ness Monster.

So, seldom is it easy. But if you work at it, and get your writing to go where you want it to go, it can feel incredibly rewarding. And even if, like some writers, you feel totally bummed out after completing something, that is okay too, because you have accomplished what you set out to do. (I'd suggest you cut yourself some slack and feel good about it, but that, my friend, is entirely up to you!)

3 / How the Exercises Work

The exercises in the next chapter are meant as warm ups, to get you into shape. In addition, what you write here is not for anybody's eyes but yours. The technical and creative aspects of your writing don't have to be polished. The ideas you write about and the themes you develop do not have to be ready for publication. Besides, you are following my exercises. My exercises will most likely take you places that you had not intended to go with your writing. You may not give a hoot about the content you produce.

But as you get into shape, you will be better able to move away from the exercises and start to run your own races. Because you have done the exercises here, you will feel strong and will feel like you can sustain your writing when you start to work on your material. Also, if you keep an open mind, you just might find that the exercises here will, in fact, help you discover ideas, themes and material you want to work on. In other words, you might find that the writing exercises you do here will lead you places where you want to go, or at least that you want to explore, with your writing. If so, cool. Run with it. If not, you are still working out and getting into writing shape.

Why develop ideas?

Why spend time on the writing exercises here? Why not just write what you want to write?

First, there is nothing wrong, and a lot right, with writing what you want to write. But I find that most writers have to develop a dozen (or more) solid ideas before they can determine what they want to write about.

Are you familiar with the parable of the sower in the Bible? In the parable, a farmer goes out to sow his seed. As he sowed, some of the seed fell along the road, and it was trampled under foot and the birds devoured it. Other seed fell on rocks, and as soon as plants started to grow, they withered away because they had no soil or nutrients. Other seed fell amid the thorns, and the thorns choked the fledgling plants. Other seeds fell on good ground, and grew and brought forth fruit.

If you have a solid idea, then you may already have planted your seed on good ground. You still have to cultivate and weed the plant, but the simple act of having an idea, a seed you might say, does not mean a story will grow from it. Or it might sprout and then wither. That is not writer's block. Developing ideas and planting them to see which ones grow is a normal part of the writing process.

In addition, as you write (here or on your own) you will be too close to what you produce. You won't be able to tell if you are producing a great idea, anything worth writing about in detail, until you let a few days or even weeks go by. (And I know some writers who would say that you sometimes have to let months or years go by before an idea turns into something worth pursuing.)

The writing process

When you find ideas that you want to pursue, you still have to pursue them and produce a first draft. And guess what? It may (will!) be crap. But do not get discouraged. Do not stop writing. Remember, you picked up this book because you're feeling blocked. Following the exercises in this book will get you writing. What it won't do is enable you to produce polished prose on your first attempt. No writer does that. A crappy first draft is not caused by being blocked. It is simply a part of the writing process, which goes something like this:

- **Discover an idea**, something you want to write about. If you lack ideas, this book will help you discover some ideas you may, eventually, want to write about.
- **Explore the idea** using various writing tools and exercises. If you discover an idea, or already have one, you can explore it using a number of the exercises in this book. This will help you determine if you want to pursue the idea.
- **Outline the idea**. Not every writer uses an outline, but outlines can help keep you on track. And, when you feel you are on track, that can help keep you writing.
- **Write a first draft**. You will not produce a first draft of everything you write, but when you find an idea that motivates you, you can often push it until you have completed a first draft.
- **Put the first draft aside**. It can be difficult to judge a first draft right after you've completed it. Putting it aside buys you some time and distance and lets you come back and see the work in a new light, which helps you decide if you want to carry on.
- **Write a second (third, fourth…) draft**. It is not unusual to produce several drafts of a work before you get feedback on it to help you determine if you should pursue publishing the work.
- **Produce a final (but not your last) draft**. Writers often workshop manuscripts and, based on the feedback, produce a final draft. Or, based on feedback, they will write several more drafts before they reach the final *final* draft.
- **Copy edit the book**. At this point, the book feels finished. It helps to have a copy editor look at it to ensure the writing is as strong as it can be and that the book unfolds in a logical (or illogical, depending on what you are trying to accomplish) manner.

- **Proofread the book**. Look where proofreading comes in the writing process. If you haven't completed your first draft and you are checking spelling and grammar, you are, in effect, procrastinating. Spelling and grammar count. (If you spot typos in this book, as I'm sure you will, email me and let me know and I will fix them in the next edition, thanks!) But at least produce a first and second draft before you start tinkering with spelling and grammar.

What you should be interested in, after completing your first draft, are big picture issues. Does the plot work and make sense? Do the characters feel real? Is the overall writing as emotionally strong as it can be?

Obviously, the exercises in this book will not take you through the entire writing process. They will, I hope, help you find and explore new ideas that you want to develop, or help you grow and discover more about ideas that you already have. And of course I hope they get you writing and help keep you writing.

Writer's Journal

Since you will be writing while reading this book, I suggest you start a writer's journal, using either a notebook or a specific file on your computer. Whatever the case, it should be an easily accessible place where you can write as you work your way through the book.

Your writer's journal is where you write notes, observations and reactions, and the place where you do your journal exercises. It is your safe place. It is not a diary. It is you being engaged in the creative process, warts and all, as you break through your block. It is you playing in your writing sandbox. It is not for public consumption, so have fun in your journal, and don't censor (or block) yourself.

Does that mean anything goes in your writer's journal? Yes! Why not? *It's for your eyes only*. Enough said.

Writing regularly makes a difference. Try to write in your journal for 15 or more minutes a day, at least three days per week. Simply use what you learn—particularly freefall and clustering (described in upcoming chapters)—to write on a regular basis in your journal.

Making writing part of your daily routine will improve your ability to write. It will also help you establish the discipline that is required if you are to continue to write once you finish this book. And it will help you discover and explore ideas that you can expand upon, if it seems appropriate to do so.

When is the best time to write in your journal? Whenever you can! Only you can find (make) time to write. Perhaps you can write first thing in the morning or just before going to bed, or instead of watching the news. Skip some time that you spend on Facebook or Twitter and write instead.

Having a set time to write will help you establish writing discipline, which is important if you want to tackle larger projects after you finish reading this book. In addition, over time you may find that particular themes, ideas, settings, situations or characters appear repeatedly in your journal. These recurring themes or images may become the bones over which you layer the flesh of poetry, short stories, a novel, essays, memoirs and so on. They become your writing dog—the reason you write and keep on writing.

One last thing

One last thing, if I may. You can work through this book in chronological order, or you can cherry pick—move from chapter to chapter depending on what seems to be of greatest interest to you. However, I suggest that you read the next several chapters (up to and including Face the Blank Page) to get a feel for how the book works and for what I will be asking you to do.

At no time do you have to complete this book or follow my words or instructions exactly as spelled out. If inspiration, like lightning, strikes as you are working on an exercise, run with your inspiration. Take it as far as you can take it. If you keep on writing and never come back to this book, then my job is done. But if you lose momentum at some point, as we all do, then this book will still be here to help you kick start your writing.

5 / Getting Emotional

So, here we are. Exercise #1 is coming up in this chapter. We will soon move from reading to writing.

How do you feel as you are about to start your first exercise? Mad, sad, scared or glad? You could be feeling other emotions too, such as ambivalent or excited, but I'd suggest that mad, sad, scared or glad covers a fairly full emotional range. And that is what I want you do to here—reflect on emotions. The goal here, as with all the exercises in the book, is to get you writing. It doesn't matter if you write fact or fiction, or both, but sometimes I will ask you to start with fact. If you end up pushing it into fiction, that's cool. But often you have to find a kernel of truth, at least truth as you see it, before pushing it into fiction. The main point, though, is to start writing and to let it flow.

Speaking of letting it flow, we will look at three exercises—freefall, directed freefall and clustering—meant to get the writing flowing. But before we look at those letting-it-flow exercises, I want you to tackle emotions. At the heart of any story, there has to be an emotional truth. If readers don't connect at an emotional level with your writing, they remain disconnected and may be inclined to stop reading. So while this book is about helping you to write, and keep on writing, in some ways it might also be about getting people to read, and keep on reading, what you write.

Yes, there will be a lot of work between free flowing writing, which is what you will be doing here, and the final published product. But I am going to suggest that, if you don't produce some free flowing writing, especially when feeling blocked, it might be difficult to discover stuff (ideas) you want to write about. And if you have ideas, but are still struggling with writing, free flowing can help you kick start the writing.

So, with that in mind, if you are ready, let's go explore emotions. If you are not ready, go have a cup of tea or coffee, go for a walk, go read a book or otherwise go relax for a while. Come back when you feel you can devote an hour or so to the exercises below.

Mad, sad, scared or glad

For this exercise, I want you to write quickly. You can even write in point form. The goal is to get your thoughts down on paper as opposed to creating a major, solidly constructed opus. At the same time, at any time when you are working on an exercise, if the spirit moves you and you are inspired to work on something more formal, feel free to run with it. While the goal isn't to get you there, I wouldn't dream of holding you back either.

To begin with, whether you are working on anything in particular or not, I want you to start with *you*—your emotions—here. Later, I'll give you the exercises again with some ideas of how you might apply them to anything you are working on. So start with you, and we'll go from there.

What I want you to do here is to think back and find the first time you remember experiencing each of the following emotions: mad, sad, scared and glad.

Before you start writing, go through each emotion one at a time—mad, sad, scared and glad—and find the situation, time and place that caused you to feel each one. In other words, sit back and take a moment (if it helps, close your eyes and visualize) and paint a mental picture. Find when and where you felt each of these emotions for the first time.

- **Mad** … find the place and time when you first remember …

- **Sad** … find the place and time when you first remember …

- **Scared** … find the place and time when you first remember …

- **Glad** … find the place and time when you first remember …

Once you are there, use the questions below to help you write about each emotion. You might simply answer each question by writing in point form. You might write full sentences. You might even write several sentences in answer to each question.

There is no right or wrong way to do this. Well, not doing it would be the wrong way, I suppose. But beyond that, tackle the exercise as you see fit. As you write, try to avoid censoring yourself. This exercise is for your eyes only. The goal is to write about the emotions, not to create a polished bit of work that anyone else will read.

Mad:

- How old were you the first time you felt mad?
- Where were you when you first felt mad? Be as specific as possible.
- Who was around when you first felt mad? What was your relationship with anyone who was around?
- Who (or what) caused you to feel mad?
- Exactly what happened to make you feel mad?
- Why did it make you feel mad?
- How did your being mad manifest itself: What did you do, or not do? What did you want to do?
- What happened next …?

- And then what happened?
- And then?
- How did anyone around you act or react?
- When did the feeling end? Why? Or if it hasn't ended, why not?

Once you are done, take a break. Then, when you are ready, carry on. (If you are writing beyond what I've suggested, no problem. This applies to all exercises. End when you want to end; carry on if so inspired. If you are finished, no problem. **So if you are ready …)**

Sad:

- How old were you the first time you felt sad?
- Where were you when you first felt sad? Be as specific as possible.
- Who was around when you first felt sad? What was your relationship with anyone who was around?
- Who (or what) caused you to feel sad?
- Exactly what happened to make you feel sad?
- Why did it make you feel sad?
- How did your sadness manifest itself: What did you do, or not do? What did you want to do?
- What happened next …?
- And then what happened?
- And then?
- How did anyone around you act or react?
- When did the feeling end? Why? Or if it hasn't ended, why not?

Once you are done, take a break. When ready, carry on.

Scared:

- How old were you the first time you felt scared?
- Where were you when you first felt scared? Be as specific as possible.
- Who was around when you first felt scared? What was your relationship with anyone who was around?
- Who (or what) caused you to feel scared?
- Exactly what happened to make you feel scared?
- Why did it make you feel scared?
- How did your fear manifest itself: What did you do, or not do? What did you want to do?
- What happened next ...?
- And then what happened?
- And then?
- How did anyone around you act or react?
- When did the feeling end? Why? Or if it hasn't ended, why not?

Done? Take a break. Then, when ready, carry on....

Glad:

- How old were you the first time you felt glad?
- Where were you when you first felt glad? Be as specific as possible.
- Who was around when you first felt glad? What was your relationship with anyone who was around?
- Who (or what) caused you to feel glad?
- Exactly what happened to make you feel glad?
- Why did it make you feel glad?
- How did your happiness manifest itself: What did you do, or not do? What did you want to do?
- What happened next ...?
- And then what happened?
- And then?

- How did anyone around you act or react?
- When did the feeling end? Why? Or if it hasn't ended, why not?

And stop. Unless, of course, you want to keep on writing.

What have we accomplished here? Something? Nothing? A lot? A little?

Our goal throughout this book is simply to do some writing—to see that we have the ability to write over, around and through whatever may be blocking us. You may not have produced anything you want to continue writing about. You may not have written how you want to write. But that's not the point. The point is to write no matter what, and to be open to where your work may (or may not) lead you. Also, you want to let the writing you do here help you turn to (or return to) your own projects by showing you that you can write. But, and this is important, there is no need to rush off to do your own thing. You are only one exercise into the book. So be patient. And keep on writing.

But before you keep on writing, feel free to take a break.

Apply emotions to your characters

Once you have taken a break, feel free to apply the above exercise to any characters in anything you might have been working on. For instance, you can apply them to the main character(s) of a story or novel you were working on. Even if you only have an idea for a story, you can apply the exercises to characters you have barely written about.

If you are working on something more personal, you might want to apply the exercises to others in your life. Doing so might require a great deal of speculation on your part, but there is nothing wrong with that, especially when you are simply trying to write. At the same time, if the exercise feels germane to any fact-based work you aspire to write, you might actually want to get people to help answer the questions for you, which would give you more background material to work with. But before we run off and interview people, let's apply the exercise to fictional characters or use speculation to apply the exercise to anyone you might want to write about.

So how do you apply the exercise to fictional (or factual) characters? We'll go through one exercise, and then you can redo it by replacing the emotional word in the exercise below with the other emotions.

One last note before we write. You could be working on fiction and you might be thinking, who cares about any of this because my char-acters are adults; their childhood emotions don't come into play. And you may be right. At the same time, as author, you should know your characters, even your secondary characters, more intimately than your readers will ever know them. (That's why we'll do more detailed character exercises later in the book.)

Also, you might surprise yourself and find grounds for using some of what you discover about your characters by going through this exercise in whatever it is you are writing. What you discover by applying this exercise to fictional characters could be the spark to get you writing again. When you discover new character aspects, you may discover possible new directions in which to take your story.

Robert Frost wrote, "No tears in the writer, no tears in the reader. No surprise in the writer, no surprise in the reader." I'm not saying you have to cry for this exercise to be effective; I am saying you might delightfully surprise yourself in terms of what you discover about your characters. You might even discover something that drives or motivate your characters and makes them tick. This is a good thing to know. And, if it fits, you could even discover flashback scenes for some of your characters.

So, simply put, run through the exercise again, only this time, do it for each of the main characters (or all the characters) in your work of fiction, or for people you are writing about in your work of non-fiction.

To get focused, jot down the names of the main characters who populate whatever it is you are working on or would like to work on. Once you have the names down on paper, do some visualization: think (don't write) about each character. Think about the first time each of your characters felt mad, sad, scared and glad. Once you have thought through each character, use the questions below to help you write about each of the emotions for each of the characters.

You might simply answer each question by writing in point form. You might write full sentences. You might even write paragraphs. The goal is to find and write about the emotions, not create polished work.

Mad—Character Name:

- How old was <*Character Name*> the first time he/she felt mad?
- Where was <*Character Name*> the first he/she felt mad? Be as specific as possible.
- Who was <*Character Name*> around the first he/she felt mad? What was <*Character Name's*> relationship with anyone who was around?
- Exactly what happened to make <*Character Name*> feel mad?
- Why did it make <*Character Name*> feel mad?
- How did the madness (anger) manifest itself: What did <*Character Name*> do, or not do? What did <*Character Name*> want to do?
- What happened next …?
- And then what happened?
- And then?
- How did anyone around act or react?
- When did the feeling end? Why? Or if it hasn't ended, why not?

Take a break, and then go through the exercise for sad, scared and glad for your first character. Then go through exercise for mad, sad, scared and glad for each of the main characters (or all of the characters) in your work, be it fiction or non-fiction. Then take a break before moving on to face the blank page in the next few chapters.

6 / Face the Blank Page: Freefall

Getting started

This chapter will introduce you freefall (stream of consciousness)—a writing exercise to help you face the blank page and overcome any inhibitions or blocks when doing so. In addition, it will help you separate your creative self from your internal editor, who causes more blockages than anyone I know. But more on how to do that, and the importance of doing it, later. First, let's start with a few...

...Words for thought

If you are having difficulty getting started or sustaining your writing, you might find of interest the following words from Diane Baker Mason, author of *Last Summer at Barebones* and several other novels:

> There was a time when I suffered from writer's block. I didn't write for many years after my teens. I always wanted to write, but it was scary. After years and years of not writing, I thought that if I couldn't be another T. S. Eliot, there was no point in writing. I was wrong. If there is any advice I can offer writers, it is this: enjoy writing, don't give up, and don't get your knickers in a knot. There will be times when you will just hate it.
>
> I owe much of my success to Atkinson College English professor Stanley Fefferman. When I first went to his class, I thought, he's going to teach me how to write a short story. What he told me instead

> was to put a pen on the paper and just write. He made it feel like such an ordinary and gentle process.

That is what writing can and should be—a gentle process. Diane published her first novel, *Last Summer at Barebones*, in 2001 at the age of 42. You can read more about her novel at dianebakermason.com.

Freefall and censorship

Freefall can help writers overcome self-censorship. Judging your own writing as you put it down (or worse, before you put it down), often causes writer's block.

While many writers start editing too early in the writing process (as mentioned earlier, proofreading is something you should leave to the end of the process), some writers never get to do any editing because they do very little writing. They censor their ideas before they begin to write. While there are many complex reasons for this, the exercises in this book are here to help you create without censoring yourself.

Your writer's journal is your safe place, the place to play with your writing. Use it and have fun as you progress through the book. Don't feel as if you have to have all the facts before you can put pen to paper, or that you have to be careful about what you say. Your journal is for your eyes only, so write in it the way a child acts, speaks and plays—uncensored. Or, as Stephen King explains in *On Writing*:

> Never look at a reference book while doing a first draft. You want to write a story? Fine. Put away your dictionary, your encyclopaedias, your World Almanac and your Thesaurus.... You think you might have misspelled a word? Okay, so here's your choice: either look it up in the dictionary to make sure you have it right—and break your

train of thought—or spell it phonetically and correct it later. Why not? Do you think the word is going to go away? When you sit down to write, write. Don't do anything else except go to the bathroom, and only do that if it absolutely cannot be put off.

Undirected freefall

With King's words in mind, we are going to look at a creative writing exercise called undirected freefall or freefall for short. This particular form of freefall is also called stream of consciousness writing or writing without a parachute.

When you freefall, you literally write without stopping for five minutes or more. Think of yourself as an artist practicing gesture sketching (rapidly drawing lines or "gestures" that do not necessarily become pictures, but enable the artist to play and experiment with lines that he or she might later incorporate in pictures).

You don't have to have anything in particular, or at all, to write about. You just put pen to paper (or fingers to keyboard) and write, write, write... If you use the keyboard, open a word processing file, position your cursor, then turn off the monitor (or lower the display on a laptop) before you begin typing, and write, write, write…

Don't stop... No matter what. Tap into the thought stream that is flowing through your mind. It is there even as you are reading this. Hear it rushing through your mind as you read? And write... write... write.... If you feel yourself coming to a halt, then doodle or use ellipsis (...) until you tap back into the stream, and write….

Do not stop to correct spelling or grammar. Do not stop to reflect upon your work or to find any facts or figures. Don't even pause to think about any facts or figures or anything that will make your work more accurate. .

It can feel unusual to write when you think you have nothing to say, or to continue to write when you know you have made a typo or grammatical error, but that is the whole point: *To jump into the stream and let the current take you somewhere, anywhere or nowhere.*

Freefall is a technique you should employ on a regular basis when writing in your journal. If you try it and stumble, get back up and carry on. It can take a bit of getting used to, writing without stopping, although you will probably take to it like a fish to water (or any other cliché you can think of when you are freefalling and the perfect analogy does not come immediately to mind).

Journal exercise: undirected freefall

What I suggest you do now is sit comfortably someplace where you will not be interrupted for the next while, and write for five or ten minutes.... Or until you feel you've reached the end of whatever comes out....

I want to stress here that your freefall does not have to be a straight narrative. Have fun. Play. Experiment. Push your personal boundaries. If you latch on to something that feels like a "story," run with it. But do not try to impose form or narrative on your freefall. Write fast. Do not pause. There will be other exercises in this book to help you shape your freefalls. But for now just play with it in the privacy of your journal.

Simply pick up your pen (recommended) or open a new page in your word processor and start wherever you start...

And don't end until you end....

If you are not ready to freefall: Go have a cup of tea, go for a stroll, go pet your dog or cat or talk to your bird... But don't put off starting for too long, unless you are right now going to work or to sleep, or your house is on fire.

When ready, just start writing... Begin your freefall and write. Go on ... write ... write ... write ...

**When you have completed your first freefall,
continue to read.**

Freefall purpose

Is there a point or purpose to freefall? Is there a point or purpose to all the gesture sketching an artist does, the voice exercises a singer does, the stretching a runner does? As mentioned previously, there is. This is your warm-up. This is you getting in shape. This is you writing for the sake of writing. This is you in a no-pressure, not-for-publication situation discovering the joy of writing and smashing through whatever it is that might be blocking you.

You can do this. All you have to do is put pen to paper, or fingers to keyboard, and write. Give it an honest effort or a couple of honest efforts.

In fact, before you go to the next chapter, try another freefall.

And don't forget to freefall regularly. Try them at different times during the day or while sitting in different locations—when you are on your own and when there are people milling about. Try them when you are surrounded by silence or when there is music playing. Try them when you are feeling up, down, bored, elated. Eventually, you might settle into a best time to freefall. The important thing is that you find about 15 minutes several days a week and freefall in your journal. Make doing so part of your writing routine!

Even as you are working on other exercises in this book continue to freefall. You never know what will come up, what you will latch on to that you can convert into who knows what. At this point, we don't care what. We just want to write and have a bit of fun doing it. That is all. Full stop.

So, when you are ready, begin your second freefall....

Please complete your freefall before you read on.

7 / Face Blank Page: Directed Freefall

Getting started

Do you have time to write? Time is there. It's yours to use, but the question is: How do you want to use it? If you are having difficulty with time, look at what you do with your time, and see what you can cut back on, or cut out.

Instead of reading the newspaper every day, read the newspaper every second or third day. Cut out a TV program. Spend less time online, on Facebook or Twitter or simply surfing the Web. Go to bed 20 minutes earlier than usual and use the time for writing. Wake up 20 minutes earlier than usual... You get the picture.

So, how was freefall? Liberating or frustrating? Either way, don't be concerned. The way you feel about it can change like the weather. The important thing to do is this: Freefall in your journal on a regular basis.

You will be amazed at what comes up, the material that floats to the surface that you can later analyse and perhaps use in (or to start) stories, poems or other writing. In addition, freefalling on a regular basis will make you a better writer. It's like working out. It helps get you ready to run a race or move a piano when the time comes to run a race or move a piano. Or write a short story. Or novel.

So stick with it. We use freefall as part of other writing exercises, including...

...Directed freefall

Directed freefall works in a manner similar to freefall, only you have a beginning—something to start the stream flowing.

You can find directed freefall "beginnings" almost anywhere: a phrase on the radio, a sentence in a newspaper, website or book, a line from a poem, a snippet of overheard conversation and so on.

The first line sometimes imposes structure on a directed freefall passage. But not always. Sometimes it inspires. But not always. Sometimes it is a relief to have somewhere to start; sometimes it feels like you are shackled. It doesn't matter. Once again, the point is to just write for the sake of writing.

Journal exercise: directed freefall

Again, think of yourself as an artist practicing gesture sketching. Play and experiment. This time you have a first line and it may influence your first few gestures. Or not. This is, after all, freefall. You do not have to create stories here. Just write. Once you get started, don't stop. You're off to the races and you don't stop until you collapse in an exhausted heap.

When you are ready to write, write down the line below, and then begin your freefall and write for five or ten minutes....

It took me a long time to....

When you have completed your directed freefall, continue reading the chapter.

When you have completed your directed freefall, take a short break. When you are ready, jot down the line below and start a second directed freefall...

Mimi watched as the birds...

When you have completed your second directed freefall, continue reading the chapter.

When you have completed your directed freefall, take a short break. When you are ready, jot down the line below and start a final (for now) directed freefall...

In the old woman's face I saw...

When you have completed your third directed freefall, continue reading the chapter.

Freefall regularly

So, how was the directed freefall? Liberating or frustrating? Different or similar to undirected freefall? Try both daily. (There are suggested directed freefall opening lines at the end of this chapter.) You may determine that one works for you, the other doesn't. Or you may find it enjoyable to use undirected freefall in the morning when you are trying to wake up your brain or in the evening when you are trying to empty it of the stuff you cram into your cranium during the day. You might use directed freefall when you feel you have a place to start or overhear a great line you cannot resist playing with or when you find a line in your undirected freefall you wish to explore further.

You can also use either to help you work on anything you want to work on. Just start, even if you don't think you have a place to start, and write freely. Or if you have an idea or opening line, jot down your thought or line and run with it. Don't be concerned if what ends up on the page is not perfect. Remember, writing is a process. There will be time to review what you've written later. There will be time to edit it later. What you want to do first is get something down on the page.

With that in mind, play with both directed and undirected freefall in your writer's journal on a regular basis. The goal is to see where the exercises take you, to have fun, to play, to be silly or super-serious, to create for the sake of creating. To see what comes up and what develops over time.

As you freefall, you may notice the appearance of certain recurring themes and images. I am not going to play pop-psychologist and tell you that your subconscious self is attempting to communicate with your conscious self. (Although that might be what is happening, but I'm not going to tell you that.) Instead, allow me to say that your writing voice is trying to break through. And it is important to listen to the voice, to liberate the voice, if you want to liberate your writing.

Does that mean if science fiction themes do not bubble up to the surface, you cannot write science fiction? Absolutely not. You can apply freefall (and other writing exercises in this book) to any genre. The way themes and images that surface in freefall make it into your writing, no matter the genre you tackle, may surprise you. So listen to the voice. Learn how to cultivate and nurture it rather than suppress it. Enjoy where it takes you at this stage of your writing.

Does that mean you must use everything that comes up? Absolutely not. You might use some of what you write, but certainly not all of it. And that's perfectly all right. As I said earlier, writing is a process, and at this point, you should be having fun creating. As you create, do not concern yourself with grammar and spelling. When you finish a freefall, put your work away for a while. When you pick it up again, look for lines, ideas, themes or characters that you find interesting or intriguing. This may be material you want to develop as you progress through the book. Or not.

The goal here is to plant a thousand seeds to see what blooms. You cultivate the seeds that bloom over time. The rest of your writing is stretching and exercising. It's gesture sketching. Most gesture sketches are tossed, but the artist is a better, stronger more creative person for having done the exercises.

So every day, try a few undirected and directed freefalls. If you find something that excites you, that you want to develop, cultivate, polish... feel free. If something overwhelms you and you want to run with it, do so. You can always come back to the book later.

Directed freefall lines to keep you going

If you enjoyed directed freefall, you might appreciate the list of directed freefall lines below. They are meant to get you started and keep you going. Feel free to play with them. But don't forget to search for your own opening lines as well.

Additional directed freefall lines:

- Looking through the scrapbook of my childhood...
- I never thought it would happen to me...
- Mimi watched as the birds...
- On the street where I grew up...
- In the old woman's face I saw...
- The last thing I remember...
- Whenever I see snow...
- "*&%$#@*^$!"...
- The first time that...
- What I really wanted was...
- Nothing looked familiar to...
- I write because...
- Terry took a deep breath before...
- In a dusty box in the basement there is...
- Chris looked out the window and...
- "Yes she was pretty, but just not her face..."
- In my mother's favourite story about me...
- I resent it when...
- It was raining the day that...
- You're not going to like this, but...
- While boiling Fred's hat in the pasta sauce, Mary thought....
- An eerie mist clung to the city...
- Chris was determined to...
- I tripped, I fell, I missed the ground...

- "You're kidding? Right? You're not...."
- I felt it, a presence, behind me...
- Fifteen minutes is all I have...
- "Can you help me?" Rae asked the stranger...
- This is where it happened, officer...
- Looking back over my life, I see....
- In my mother's hands, I see...
- Terry place the flower on the casket and....
- Coming at me, the tree and the purple cow....

8 / Clustering (Word Association)

Getting started

So far, you've experienced two writing exercises meant to get you started and to help you sustain your writing. Freefalling regularly should help you overcome the voice of the internal censor who says spelling and grammar are paramount, which gets in the way of creativity and can cause you to write in fits and starts or worse, cause you to stop writing. Spelling and grammar count, but who cares about spelling and grammar when you are having a private moment in your journal or when you are on a creative roll.

Editing and revision have their places—after you have had fun inventing and creating. You don't have to buy into that philosophy, but I urge you to try to separate your creator from your editor and see how it goes. I find it brings much more joy to my writing. In fact, I was seldom able to complete a first draft of a short story until I separated the two. With that in mind, I am going to introduce you to an internal research exercise known as clustering (also known as brainstorming, mind mapping and word association), to further spark your creativity. Before we try clustering, how about a few...

...Words for thought

Here are a few words on writing that I'd like to share with you.

> What the writer often lacks is not ideas but a means of getting in touch with them. – Gabriele Rico

Internal research, using the techniques presented in the next couple of chapters, will enable you to get in touch with your idea seeds. Once planted, they can blossom into amazing passages of writing. Not every seed will blossom. Nor should they. Your job is to cultivate and nurture the seeds that seem healthiest.

> Little children can create wonderful, uninhibited stories full of fanciful characters. But as the years pass, the regimens of school and community kill the storyteller that lives within each of us. To write fiction, you have to dig deep and discover that story-teller. – W. P. Kinsella

Write like a child and rediscover your storyteller. Go exploring. See what happens. It's a great way to break through blocks. Revision/editing—correcting spelling, grammar, refining the plot, choosing more powerful words and developing characters more fully—occurs later, after creation. Of course, you are not doing anything wrong if you develop your characters or outline your plot before you write a story or novel. Some prolific authors will tell you to never begin anything without an outline. However, before you get to the outline stage you need to do some brainstorming. You also need to feel comfortable with letting your writing flow (a state that freefall allows you to achieve) before you plunge into any serious creation, no matter how fully developed your characters are or how fully outlined your plot is.

With that in mind, let's move on to...

...Clustering

Clustering is a form of word association or brainstorming that helps you conduct your internal research before you create. It enables you to put on paper all you know about a topic and all you associate with a topic before you write about it. It helps you get your knowledge out in the open and lets you focus on creation by reducing the time you spend pondering your subject matter as you write.

It also sparks writing ideas because, as you cluster, your mind makes associations and produces images that it would have not have otherwise produced. And these ideas/associations can help enrich your writing.

To cluster, you write a key word or phrase in the middle of a page, underline it and circle it. (See the example of clustering below.) You then draw a dash from the circle and write down the first word or phrase you associate with the key word and circle the new word or phrase.

Then you draw a line from the newly circled word and write down the first word or phrase you associate with it. You circle that word or phrase and continue.

The lines and circles are meant to spark the creative side of your brain, so keep on going until you feel that the word association string has come to an end. Once that happens, go back to your key word, draw another line from it, and write down the next word or phrase that comes to mind and carry on again. Soon you will have on your page something that looks like a messy spider's web filled with words and phrases.

Keep on clustering until you come to a natural end. You may have two association strings; you may have 22 or more strings. There is no right or wrong amount. You simply end when you end.

(See Clustering example on the next page.)

CLUSTERING
CHUNKS
THOUGHTS
IDEAS
FLAMES
SPARKS
INTERNAL
EXTERNAL
OTHER SOURCES
RESEARCH
LEFT BRAIN
RIGHT BRAIN
LINEAR
OUTLINE
BLANK PAGE
STARTING POINT
WORD ASSOCIATION
BRAINSTORMING
MINDMAPPING
TREASURE HUNT
GOLD
WORDS
PHRASES
IMAGES
METAPHORS
PREWRITING
INFORMATION
DATA CHUNKS
OUTLINE
ONE BITE AT A TIME
APPLE

Journal exercise

What do you do with your cluster? We'll discuss that in the next Chapter. For now, however, I'd like you to try another journal exercise. Before you cluster, read the above instructions again. Once you are ready, cluster the word below.

Key Word: to cluster: *HEART*

When you have completed your cluster, continue reading the chapter.

Clustering and freefall in harmony

So, how was clustering? Were you surprised by what came up? Pleased, delighted, concerned, angered? Frustrated? Try to cluster other words or phrases. There are more key words in this chapter that you can use but feel free to come up with your own key words as well. The point is to use clustering to go exploring before you write. We will soon look at how you can use it to help you write, too.

Use your writer's journal as a place to cluster and freefall on a regular basis. You may be amazed at the material that floats to the surface—material that you can later analyse and perhaps use in stories, poems or other writing. And if you're looking for a way to use clustering outside of creative writing, try it the next time you have to write an article, essay, memo or report. Pick a key word that relates to whatever you have to write about and cluster. Clustering will help you get down on paper everything you associate with the topic (and then some) before you start to write. It is an excellent pre-writing exercise.

Journal exercise

I'd like you to cluster another word. This time, I want you to try something a little different. The clustering process is the same: Write down your key word, draw a circle around it, draw a line from it and write your next word. Circle it, draw a line...

However, when you finish your clustering, flip into freefall.

How do you know you have finished your clustering? You will feel it. You will feel the urge to write. You will resist the urge at first, but at some point you will end your cluster and start to freefall....

Let the cluster inspire your freefall; however, continue to freefall without censoring yourself. You do not have to include in the freefall all the words and phrases of you cluster, but if you feel the freefall slowing down, glance at your cluster for inspiration. After all, the cluster contains all the words and phrases you associate with the key word. And what is creative writing but a collection of words, phrases, images, metaphors (sentence, paragraphs, chapters or stanzas) associated with central themes, plots and characters?

So, if you are ready, write down the key word below and begin your cluster... (Don't forget to flip into freefall when you feel the urge to write. Write freely, without censoring yourself. But if you find your writing coming to an end, look to your cluster strings for inspiration or for a word or phrase to help you keep on writing.)

Key Word: to cluster: *HELP*

When you have completed your cluster, read on.

Supplementary clustering material

Below are a number of words you can use for clustering. Before you move on, try at least one or two more cluster/freefall combinations. Chose words from the list that resonate with you or pick your own words or phrases. Don't forget to flip into freefall when you complete your cluster. Add clustering to your journaling arsenal.

Additional clustering key words

• Letting go	• Feast
• Needles	• Going Away
• Fish	• Lilacs
• Apple	• Horse
• Christmas	• Home
• Cat	• Writing
• Dog	• Boundary
• Woods	• Knife
• Beach	• Sunset
• Happy	• Hands
• Love	• Sky
• School	• Breakfast
• Fist fight	• Alone
• Marbles	• Work
• Mud	• Chocolate
• Games	• Church
• Skating	• Lover
• Lost	• Trees
• Prisoner	• Sex
• Future	• Life
• Me	• Death
• Dreams	• Walk
• Friends	• Snow
• Enemy	• Ice
• Candy	• Birthday
• Puppy	• Family
• Gun	• Heaven or Hell
• Old woman	• God (or your personal deity)

Additional clustering exercises

- Cluster each member of your family.
- Cluster each room in the house where you grew up.

- Cluster words or phrases that have meaning to you.

Don't forget to flip into freefall when you complete your clusters. It's a great way to explore themes, ideas, situations, characters and so on. Again, the goal is to plant idea seeds to see what comes up. If, however, you plant a seed and it blooms immediately, pursue it. But don't fret if you feel as if you are doing a lot of gesture sketching. You are writing. Be like a child exploring a new place or revisiting a favourite place and have fun with it.

Clustering to break blocks

If you have been working on something and have been feeling blocked, you can use clustering to help break through your block. Here are a couple of ways you can use it to help kick start your writing. What you want to do is to come up with a key word or phrase that represents an aspect of what you are working on. It can be the title of the work, if you've given it a title. It can be a phrase that represents a key element of the plot or the theme of your work. It can be something that you associate with the work. What you choose is less important than making a choice.

You then cluster the word or phrase you have selected. Try to give it a solid cluster workout. In fact, feel free to use a sheet of paper that is larger than the standard 8.5 by 11-inch sheet of paper. That way you will be mentally prepared to fill a larger space with your cluster. Failing that, make sure you have several sheets of paper handy. If you fill one sheet, move on to another.

Once you've done your cluster, flip into freefall and see where it takes you.

If that sounds a bit too opened ended for you, no problem. If you are working on something in particular and are feeling blocked, you can cluster something about the point where you are blocked. It could be that an idea no longer seems as fully developed as it was when you began. It could be that you are stuck on a plot point. It might be that you are having problems with a character or the relationship between two characters. All of that is fodder for clustering. It's up to you to come up with what you want to cluster. Cluster a key word or phrase that represents what is blocking you, and then freefall on the subject, once you have completed your clustering.

Go forth and try it, and see where it takes you. Or simply carry on with the exercises in the book if you are not quite ready to plunge into something that you are working on or want to work on. There will be time for that later.

9 / Why Change?

I want you to look at several of your cluster/freefalls from the previous chapter (or other cluster/freefalls or directed or undirected freefalls you have done). Pick one or two that feel the most inspired, closest to your heart, or closest to what you want to accomplish with your writing and look at the first half a dozen sentences or the first paragraph of your freefall. Copy the first few sentences or the first paragraph or two of your freefall and paste this beginning at the end of the freefall. (Or if you are using a journal, rewrite your beginning at the end of the freefall.)

All will be made clear below. For now, go with the flow.

Why am I asking you to look at where your freefalls started and then copy and paste the beginnings at the end? Often, short stories, poems, even novels, end near to where they began. Notice I said near, not in the same place. Between the beginning and end, some movement or change occurs in the character(s) and the situation. Perhaps the main character has a better understanding of himself/herself, his/her past or present in relation to the past, or has resolved a major issue that occurred early on in the story.... Whatever. The important point is this: *Change has occurred.*

I call that the *delta factor*. Delta or Δ (the triangle symbol) is used in mathematics to represent change. And that's what your stories need: change. In other words, where you end up must be different from where you began, but it must also be connected to where you began.

Having said that, your story can start at the end, and then you can take the reader on a journey that shows how your story (your main character) arrived at that end. Yet somehow that end must be different than the end at the beginning. Otherwise, what was the journey all about?

In fact, you can start anywhere and end anywhere. The important thing is that something has changed and the reader gets it (or doesn't get it, but not because there is nothing to get).

If you want to watch a movie that plays on narrative time convention (and if you don't mind swearing and violence) rent *Pulp Fiction*. When you get to the end of the movie, you will realize that the movie actually ends about one-third of the way through the lives of the characters. You will see, at the end of the movie, that one character is about to change and the other one isn't (which leads to his death half way through the movie). Confusing? Not if the story is told, and structured, well.

And in the end...

But I digress. Let's get back to writing, with a delta example. A creative writing student once submitted a cluster-based freefall ("woods" was the key word) that began:

> In the woods I walk. I inhale the dampness of the earth—a peculiar, musky smell. True nature's ripe aroma. Following the trail through thick, green foliage, I see trillium flowers blooming in the shadows. Sunlight seeps through the broad branches, which shelters the flowers and damp earth. In the shadows are all these bugs. Biters. I want to commune with nature, but think I am lost. All I can do is rush headlong through the woods and swat wildly as clouds of bugs descend...

In the freefall, the narrator goes through a horrible time with the bugs. Gets more lost. Hears eerie sounds and fantasizes about strange creatures in the woods. She falls asleep at one point but a squirrel drops an acorn on her head, which hurts but wakes her from her reverie. Then she sees a deer and fawn in a clearing. It's a magical moment. She watches as they eat the damp foliage, then dart off. As she tries to follow them, she discovers where she is, figures out her way home and soon emerges from the woods.

The story ended there, with her emerging into the sunshine. I asked her to paste her opening paragraph on to the end, reread her story and then edit the opening that she had pasted at the end. This is how the revised story *ended*:

> Out of the woods I walk, no longer stumbling through thick foliage. No longer enveloped by the scent of raw earth. The imagined sounds are already faded; the buzzing bugs barely a memory. But I carry with me my mementoes—a bump on the head from the acorn dropped by the squirrel and the vision of deer and her fawn that I will never forget.

Notice how "out of the woods" parallels the "into the woods" opening? What she did here was more than paste the beginning at the end. She let the beginning inspire the end. She rewrote the beginning at the end and demonstrated that change had occurred—a change that reflected where the story began but was somehow different because of all that had gone on.

Do all stories have to reflect their opening lines? No. Not all. But there needs to be change. Pasting your beginning at the end is one way of ensuring change happens. Sometimes when you do this, it will inspire you to edit other aspects of the story—even the beginning—so you can get to the point where you decided to end it.

I often find that the process of pasting my beginning at the end, and then revising it, actually helps me edit my beginning.

You see, once I have a better sense of where my story should end and of what change has occurred, I can then ask myself if my story has started where it should have started. It's as if once I know where the story truly ends, I can discover where it should actually begin. I hope this doesn't seem too convoluted. The fact is, any writing needs to be edited and this is one way of having your creative self work hand-in-hand with your internal editor—instead of being at odds with the editor.

It is this change (the delta factor) that makes the story work. It is the change that makes the reader say, "I get it!" The point, theme, purpose, meaning (or "whatever") of the story (or poem) is often found in the change that takes place between the Alpha (beginning) and Omega (end).

Delta and writer's block

So what does all of this have to do with writer's block? It all depends on what your block is. If you are not writing at all, it may have nothing to do with writer's block. However, if you are having difficulty finishing a piece, this exercise might help you get back to writing.

Imagine if I gave you some darts and said, "Let's see if you can hit the target" but I didn't tell you where the target was. No matter how hard you tried, I think it would be impossible to hit the target. When you copy the beginning of your work and paste it at the end, you might reconnect to where you began and might see where you need to (want to) go with your story. In other words, the beginning pasted at the end might give you a target or destination, and that might help you plunge back into the story and start to write, with your target or destination in mind.

The hope is that this technique will help rekindle your connection with your work, rekindle the excitement (and the idea) that caused you to plunge into it in the first place. But even if you are not working on anything in particular right now, or are not blocked by a missing ending, try the journal exercises below to see how this technique can help you push a story to the end.

Journal exercise

Before you read on, pick at least one freefall (freefall, directed freefall or cluster-inspired freefall) and paste the beginning at the end. Read what you have written again. Decide if or how you want to change the pasted-on ending. Or perhaps you want to change the beginning and new ending. Play with it. Not too much. Not for too long (unless you are having fun with it).

In other words, you don't have to try to turn what you've written into a fully edited short story. It may be you've written an extended anecdote, the beginning of a personal essay or simply a descriptive passage. What I want you to do is think about the opening and the ending of whatever it is you wrote, and see if you can ensure there is a delta factor—change—between where your writing opens and where it ends. Try this process several times, with different freefall passages and see where it goes. And if you are having difficulty ending something that you have written, try this exercise to see if it helps you find an ending for your work.

When you have completed your delta factor exercise, continue with the chapter.

Editor's job

As we can see, one of the editor's jobs is to ask: Does this story start where it should? Does it end where it should? But to do that the editor has to have some raw material to work with. The raw material is the freefall you have created.

When reading over a first draft, the editor asks: What has happened here? What has changed during the course of the story? What hasn't changed? What could or should change. What shouldn't? Why? Why not?

It is the editor's job to look at creation analytically and to help you reach conclusions about what should or shouldn't be done with the work to move it forward and make it more complete. Yes, some editors (perhaps unruly from their banishment from the creative process) might work to sabotage you by giving you nothing but negative feedback. However, when you constructively edit your work, you will be able to more easily discern which of your creations you should move forward with, and that will help you overcome blocks that may prevent you from finishing a solid first draft of something you are working on.

Suddenly it's not such a big deal that of all the seeds you planted only two or three feel as if they are about to bloom. Sometimes you don't see the potential in your work right way. The passage of time (and your internal editor) can, at times, help you determine what will and what will not bloom.

As Natalie Goldberg, author of *Writing Down the Bones*, says:

> Every time we begin writing, we wonder how we did it before. Each time is a new journey with no maps. The best test of a piece of writing is over time. If you're not sure of something, put it away for a while. Look at it six months later. Things will be more clear.

Distance from your freefalls or any writing you are working on can give you (in mode as editor) perspective on your writing—help you determine what stands the (short-term) test of time and is worth keeping, worth working on, worth pushing further.

If you do feel your editor sabotaging your creative efforts early on, try telling him or her the following: "Get thee behind me, Editor." Give your raw freefalls the benefit of distance. Continue to work on freefalls and clustering until you feel your confidence in your ability to create has grown, which should help you work on your own material or convert selected work produced here into material you want to work on.

10 / Journey Through Childhood I

Getting started

Childhood is a rich source of creative ideas, and creative ideas help us break through blocks. Yes, sometimes they block us if we don't want to face our childhood. At the same time, it's a place that is rich in feelings and emotions. Facing them—the good, the bad and perhaps even the ugly—can help free us and help us face the other writing we want to do. Sometimes, facing childhood becomes part of the writing we do. After all, every character in fiction (or in memoirs) has a childhood—whether the writer delves into it or not. And every writer has a childhood, which is worth delving into, even if—especially if—the writer delves into it and fictionalizes it.

We will use a number of techniques—including freefall and clustering—to help us draw on childhood memories and experiences that can be used to find and explore ideas for writing and to infuse writing with the power of raw emotion. The focus will be on creation or writing for the sake of writing. There is no need to allow your internal editor to intrude here, while in creative mode. There will be time enough for editing when the creating is done, if you so chose to review, shape and edit anything you write here.

Words for thought

Before we begin, here are a few words that I would like to share with you:

> When I started writing I started from childhood.
> I never write about where I am right now. It takes a

> while to process events and to digest them. – Alice Munro

As Alice Munro indicates, writing is often based on reflection—looking back on events after you've had time to deal with them and digest their significance. Doing so makes you a better storyteller. Reflecting on childhood is also a great way to find and incorporate powerful emotions in your writing. And emotions make writing come alive and ring true for others. In short, a story without emotion is like a day without sunshine: dull, flat, dreary.

That doesn't mean any reader will enjoy or relate to a story just because it packs an emotional punch. Reading, and how readers react to emotion, is a very subjective experience. However, I put it to you that most readers would react with a big yawn to a story that lacked emotion.

With that in mind, here are a few more words for thought:

> I wish I had kept a diary over the years. The memory sometimes plays tricks or is forgetful, and we miss a lot of the past that could be helpful in our present. – Sidney Sheldon

> Some things you never lose no matter how long they've been gone. – Pogo

> Some people are ashamed of their past and others just write best sellers. – Anonymous

> It took me my whole life to learn how to paint like a child. – Pablo Picasso

It doesn't hurt to learn how to create with your heart on your sleeve, with the emotions of a child or an adolescent. If it all seems too extreme, you can always pull it back when you shape (edit) your story or poem. The goal now, however, is to find the things that you think you've lost (or you may have hidden or misplaced)—to connect with your past, build on it and push it somewhere strange, if you choose, called fiction, biography or even poetry.

Marcel Proust, the French novelist, is best known for *Á La Recherche Du Temps Perdu* (*Remembrance of Things Past*), his autobiographical novel told mostly in a stream-of-consciousness (freefall) style. The work collected experiences from Proust's childhood, observations of high-class lifestyle, gossip and recollections of the closed world in which the author never found his place. The key scene in the novel is when a madeleine cake (a small, rich cookie-like pastry) enables the narrator to experience the past as a simultaneous part of his present existence.

Or as Proust writes:

> And suddenly the memory revealed itself: The taste was that of the little piece of madeleine which on Sunday mornings at Combray (because on those mornings I did not go out before mass), when I went to say good morning to her in her bedroom, my aunt Léonie used to give me, dipping it first in her own cup of tea or tisane....

If cookies and tea, and the memories associated with it, can inspire a significant novel, then it might be worth your while to journey through childhood. Again, what we are going to try to do here is to create. To drop a thousand seeds and see what is worth nurturing. Remember, at this stage you are writing journal entries. You are not writing for publication. So there is no need to censor or judge yourself, which often inhibits or blocks writing. You are here to find memories, emotions and feelings. Eventually, you may choose to push some of what you find into fiction or incorporate it into something you are working on. Or not. In the meantime, enjoy the writing!

Emotions of childhood

Why are childhood emotions so powerful? Childhood is where emotions are at their rawest. Notice how quickly kids are prepared to laugh, cry, scream, or express frustration, boredom or anger... the whole emotional range. The objective here, as you write, is to get in touch with the full range or your emotional experiences so you can incorporate appropriate emotions into your work.

The exercises in this chapter are meant to help you recreate incidents from childhood, find emotions and images associated with them and use material you find as starting points for your writing. And if you find yourself exaggerating or telling lies creatively in your writing, no problem! That means you are pushing your experiences into fiction. With that in mind, here are writing exercises to help you find ideas and emotions that may be buried beneath the rubble of childhood. Try these exercises and see where they take you or where you go with them.

Journey through childhood exercises

For the purpose of the five exercises below, I define childhood as any time between birth and the age of 16. (Feel free to extend the age if appropriate.) It's possible that you'll write a lot while reading this chapter, so I suggest you pace yourself. Having said that, only you can set a pace with which you are comfortable. Do not concern yourself with editing your work. As mentioned earlier, focus on creating. Put the work away as you complete it. Come back to it after you finish reading this book and let your editor help you determine if you should pursue any of the raw work you complete here.

Exercise 1A: Possessions of Childhood

Create a list of the possessions you had as a child. List all you can remember, or focus on a particular age or age range and the possessions from that age or age range. Create your list, and then do the exercise below.

Choose one childhood possession from your list and cluster it. Once you have finished your cluster, *flip into freefall* and see where that takes you.

Once you have completed your clustering and freefall, take a break.

Exercise 1B: Possessions of Childhood

Think of one possession in particular, and use some or all lines below to help write a series of short (or long!) **directed freefalls**, starting with these lines:

- The possession I am thinking of is...
- I got it from...
- I got it when...
- And kept it for...
- I used it for...
- I kept it until...
- What it meant to me then was...
- The memories it brings back are...
- Thinking about this possession now, I feel...

Try the above two exercises with several other possessions.

Conversely, create a list of possessions that siblings or friends had. Pick one from your list and cluster it, and then flip into freefall and see where you go when writing about the possessions of others. Or apply the above directed freefall lines to a childhood possession that belonged to someone other than yourself.

When you have completed your possessions of childhood exercises, continue with the chapter.

Exercise 2: Seasons of Childhood

Many of our childhood memories are associated with seasons or holidays. For this exercise, I'd like you to **pick a specific season** (or holiday) from childhood and use the *outline* below to recreate a scene or setting. Then focus on an event or events that occurred during that time and at that place. Use the *leads* provided below the outline words to help you research the event through short bursts of directed freefall.

Outline

- Year and season (or holiday):
- The place:
- My age and school grade:
- Family members around at the time:
- Family members not around at the time:
- Friends I had then:
- Possessions related to this time and place:
- Event(s) related to this time and place:

Leads

- I have chosen to go back to this time and place because...
- One event I associate with this time and place is...
- I am thinking about this event because...
- I see... I hear... I feel... I smell... I taste... I sense...
- The dominant emotion I associate with this event is...
- If I could say one thing to someone there at the time, it would be...
- If I could say one thing to someone who was not there, I'd say...

- If this event were the basis of a story or a poem, it would be titled...

Feel free to start a new freefall once you have completed the above exercise. Run with it. See where it takes you.

When you have completed your seasons of childhood exercise, continue with the chapter.

Exercise 3: In the Home Where I Grew Up

Sit somewhere comfortable and think about a room, just one room, in the home where you grew up. You might think about several rooms at first, but I want you to close your eyes and focus on one room. Once you have picked a room on which to focus, start to recreate the room in your mind.

With your eyes shut, visualize yourself walking around the room. What do you see, hear, smell, feel, taste? Imagine yourself in the room on a specific day or at a particular time in your life. What do you see? Who else do you see? What is going on? What isn't going on?

When you open your eyes, use the leads below to help you write about what you just visualised, then flip into freefall or use the last line of the leads as the first line of a directed freefall. Alternatively, feel free to cluster—using the name of the room as your key word—and then freefall.

Leads

- The year is______
- I am _________ years old
- The room is______
- I have chosen it because...
- I look around and see...
- I also see...
- In addition, I see...

- I (hear/feel/smell/taste)...
- What I am doing there is...
- Now what happens is...
- Thinking back on what transpired in that room, I feel...

When you have completed the above exercise, continue with the chapter.

Exercise 4: Photographic Journey

Think of a favourite photograph from childhood or find an old photo to use for this exercise. If you can't picture a picture or find a photo, try to freeze a particular moment in your mind. Use the leads below to guide short directed freefall bursts.... Then write a directed freefall using the line provided below the leads, or produce your own opening line and freefall.

Leads

- I have a picture of...
- In the picture, I look...
- Also in the picture are...
- I was the kind of kid who...
- Thinking back, I remember...
- And this memory leads me to...
- The emotion I felt then was...
- The emotion I feel now is...
- If I could have this picture taken over again, I would...

Once you have completed the above, start a directed freefall using the following line:

This picture from childhood tells a story of….

When you have completed your Photographic Journey exercise, continue with the chapter.

Exercise 5: Life with Parents

Use the leads below to express childhood feelings about parents or guardians. I have primarily used the word "father" in the leads, but feel free use "mother" or a significant guardian. Or go through the exercise twice—once for the male influence and once for the female influence in your life.

Leads

- When I think of my father's life before I was born, I see a man who....
- Some of the most important experiences in his early life were....
- When I think of my father at home, I see him....
- He was the kind of father who....
- When I think of the similarities between my parents, I see....
- When I think of the differences between my parents, I see....
- Some similarities between my father and me are....
- A question I have never asked my father is....
- I would like to ask this question because....
- I would like him to answer it by saying....
- But he would probably say....
- If my father were to describe me as a child, he would say....

After completing the leads, flip into freefall. Or take a break.

When you have completed this exercise, read on.

Journal exercise

If any of the above writing exercises inspires you to explore childhood events further, use your journal to do so. You can explore events based upon the above exercises, or investigate other events inspired by these exercises or that simply pop into your mind. Use the structure of these exercises to help you on your journey. Or cluster key words and freefall.

Don't be afraid of the truth as you remember it, *but don't be afraid to push your memory into the creative lies of fiction or the shape of poetry*. In other words, use your memories as beginnings or springboards. Dive off them and see the depths to which your writing can take you.

What do you do with all the writing?

That is for you to decide. Some gesture sketches are worth framing. Others are worth exploring further. Some form the basis of the final picture. Others get tossed. As mentioned, distance (time away from your raw creation) will help you decide.

For now, though, the goal is to break through blocks—to start writing and to keep on writing. With that in mind, let's continue our journey through childhood in the next chapter. (But, as always, feel free to take a break after writing for some time. Walking away for a bit can help you recharge your creative batteries.)

11 / Journey Through Childhood II

Getting started

How was your journey though childhood? Some people have accused me of attempting to perform therapy. Nothing could be further from my intent, although there is no denying that the exercises can be cathartic, painful, enjoyable, entertaining, boring, exhilarating, and more. All those feelings are secondary to capturing and recreating emotions, which are at the heart of writing that begs to be read.

Think about how you react to what you read. Which do you prefer: flat, two-dimensional characters or fully developed characters who seem to live and breathe? I think you know my take on this, and infusing your characters—when and where appropriate in a story—with emotions that are real is one way of creating fully-developed characters. Also, once you have a sense of who your characters are, and what makes them tick, it can be easier to work with them.

Many writers are blocked because they don't know who they are working with. That doesn't mean your characters have to be you! Not at all. But the hope hear is that as you discover how emotion can make your writing come alive, and help the words to flow, you will think more about your characters, who they are and why they do what they do, and you will be able to work with them. Of course, if you are writing a memoir, an autobiography or a biography of someone you know personally, infusing your writing with emotion will make it more captivating.

Journal exercise

I'd like you to tackle one last journey through childhood exercise. Before you get to the exercise, start by reading the opening to my short story, *The Nuncles*. This story is based on several exercises. I conducted a number of clusters, freefalls, directed freefalls and character outlines (which we'll do later) to make the characters in the story as real as possible.

My short story, *The Nuncles* (published in my short story collection, *Rebel in the Back Seat* – paullima.com/books/rebel.html), is based on very real memories that I have of several of my uncles. Yes, the memory is exaggerated and pushed into fiction; however, the memory and underlying emotions are very real.

The Nuncles

> They were as tall as hydro poles, and even wider around their roll-out-the-barrel chests, the Nuncles were. Their arms were as thick as Toronto telephone books and their legs would have made elephants jealous. Their hands were always clenched in huge mallets that looked like they could bust concrete slabs into dust.
>
> The Nuncles. The three of them. Like triplet Titans. Sam, Tom and Joe. Three Nuncles … three syllables … a whole lot of shit-kicking trouble. Not quite identical, but it was difficult to tell them apart unless one had a discerning eye or the unfortunate opportunity to compare their roughly landscaped faces up close.
>
> The Nuncles would thrust out beefy drumstick fingers when they stooped to pick me up and scoop me off Grandma's Ossington Avenue porch. They held me high, as if I was a virgin they were compelled to sacrifice to the Sun. But before they tossed me salad-like into the sky, they held me close

to their crazy man-in-the-moon howling faces, pock-marked with deep, black craters and pits, and bursting with red and yellowish volcanic pustules that looked as if they would explode like Vesuvius at any moment. They did this often, which is how I learned how to tell them apart.

The Nuncles. That's what I called my triplet Italoamericani uncles. I was in awe of them; they scared this eight-year-old kid shitless.

Your turn

So those were *The Nuncles*. Now what I want you to do is to think back to childhood, perhaps between the ages of 4 to 12. Create a list of adults. Adults who frightened you. Adults who made you laugh. Adults who made you run and hide. Adults you ran to and hugged. Adults you were in awe of. Adults who inspired you or somehow moved you. Adults who, for better or for worse, were a part of your life.

Pick one adult or, if appropriate, one group of adults. Give the adult or the group a nickname, something that describes them to you. Even if you did not have a name for them as a child, even if it might not mean anything to a reader, initially, give them a nickname.

Once you have your nickname, use that name as your cluster key word, and cluster like crazy.

When you are done, when you feel you have captured every physical aspect and emotional sensation, as well as any key incidents/events in your relationship with the adult(s), flip into freefall.

When you flip into freefall, try to paint a detailed, fantastical word. Heap it on. Pile it high. Over do it. Then over do it again. And again. No holds barred. Even if your editor screams in fury at you, "Enough. Too much. Too far." Take it further then. Push it higher, wider, deeper...

Who cares what you say as you write your version of *The Nuncles*? This is for you, for your journal. Later, no rush, if you feel you have something, you can always tone it down or pull it back. Or heap more on it. That is the wonder of the writing process. Write now. Put it away. Edit later.

With that in mind, make your list of significant adults (if you have not done so already). Pick one adult or one group of adults. Assign a nickname. And...

...If you are ready, write down your key word—the nickname—and begin your cluster. (Don't forget to flip into freefall when you feel the urge to write.)

When you have completed your version of *The Nuncles* exercise, continue with the chapter.

Now what?

So what do you do with all the journey-through-childhood work that you have written? I don't believe in using definitions—defining short stories or poetry for you and then saying, "OK, based on that definition, turn what you have written into a short story or a poem." That is simply inviting the editor to impose form upon your raw research, your rough drafts, your introspection, your creative endeavours—before either you are the work is ready for form. Besides, this book is all about the joy of writing and breaking through blocks.

Ah, but publishers, editors, readers require—demand—form, you say.

And I have no problem with form. Right now, my hope is that your gestures are beginning to take shape almost organically—that you are starting to discover or rediscover your voice and create in a more confident manner. And that you are having fun! There will be ample time for revision and for imposing form later, when and if you are so inclined.

Having said that, if you have a sense of what you would like to try to do with some of your sketches, feel free. At the same time, if you want to carry on with writing exercises, please do so. There is no rush to grow up, be an adult and impose form on your work. But to help you slowly evolve in that direction, we will soon use a writing exercise called modelling to help you shape work—still without invoking the editor. We want to work within form in a way that keeps the emotional heart of your work (of your creation) beating.

Before you move on, take a moment and go back over the work you have created based on the journey through childhood exercises and review several freefalls. How interested are you in what you have written? Can you see expanding on your work? If it you feel like it, pick one piece of work that intrigues you and conduct the delta factor exercise with it. See where it goes.

Or, for now, simply read on.

12 / What If?

Do you want a cheese sandwich?

The Canadian author, Alistair McLeod (*No Great Mischief*) suggests writers should fear cheese sandwiches. Why? Imagine your reader putting down your just published novel or collection of short stories or poetry to head off to the kitchen to make... a cheese sandwich... and never returning to your book. Imagine if the allure of a bland, boring, tasteless, dull, dry cheese sandwich is more compelling than the allure of... your writing! *Ouch.*

However, before you let the fear—that a reader will replace your work with a cheese sandwich—grab you by the neck and throttle the writing life out of you, ask yourself this: What motivates the reader?

I'd suggest it is *hunger*. A hunger to be entertained or informed. Or to be informed in an entertaining manner. Or to be entertained in an informative manner. Nothing more. Nothing less. You, as writer, have no control over what motivates the reader. And you have no control over how readers will react to your writing. The reader has the right to react in any way he or she chooses based on the full range of his/her life/emotional experiences. You have no control over that. So don't try to control it. To worry and fret about the reaction of the reader before you write your book is grounds for blocking yourself before you write your book. Control your writing, instead. That is your job!

Think of the books you loved that others loathed, or the movies you loathed that others loved. When it comes to literature, or any form of entertainment, you are entering an incredibly subjective realm. In other words, develop a thick skin and expect to lose some readers to cheese sandwiches. You have no control over that. But work to make your writing as entertaining and/or informative as you can. In short, work hard at your craft. Be true to your vision. Listen to constructive feedback. Accept what makes sense; ignore the rest. The reader will do what the reader does regardless of what you do.

And if you haven't tried a Kraft processed cheese single slice on white Wonder Bread smothered with margarine in a while, give it a shot. It's not as bland as it sounds. (However, if you want to really jazz it up, add a crisp leaf of iceberg lettuce to it. Yum!)

What motivates you?

So if you do not have control over what motivates the reader, or how the reader will react to your writing, what do you have control over? Your work. And, I would suggest, your own motivation.

While I hope readers stick with my work, I would not be offended if a reader left my work behind for a cheese sandwich. I would, however, think twice about my motivation if *I* left writing behind for one. Having said that, I do stop for lunch, and sometimes lunch is rather bland—but I don't drop my writing to have bland meals. I stop writing when I am famished and need some food, any food, to refuel me so I can carry on. There is a difference!

What motivates you? Why do you write? You are part way through the book. Maybe it's a good time to think about that or even freefall about it.

Writing exercise, anyone?

If you want to try a directed freefall, here is a line to get you going:

I write because...

Or cluster the word *Motivation* and see what you come up with. Then flip into freefall.

Or cluster the phrase *cheese sandwich*. Then flip into freefall.

Or simply start writing..... Go. Write....

Come back in 10 or 15 minutes, or an hour or so, and read the rest of this Chapter. Go. Scoot. Write!

When you have completed the writing exercise, continue with the chapter.

What motivates the story?

Hope you had some motivational writing fun and perhaps gained some insight into something or into nothing at all. But guess what? What motivates you is immaterial. (*Oh, now he tells me*!) By that, I mean what motivates you to write is no doubt different from what motivates me to write, and who cares? From the perspective of the story or the reader, what does it matter why you write?

Oh, maybe one day, if (when) you become a famous writer journalists will ask. "What motivated you to write?" But that will not change one word of what you have written.

So why the previous exercise? First, I hope you found it a fun and perhaps somewhat thought-provoking writing exercise. Beyond that, it helps to be conscious of what motivates you to write so you can harness that energy—especially if you are feeling down, preoccupied or blocked. Figure out what motivates you to write and you will most likely write more often so you can reap whatever reward you reap when you write. Even if, on occasion, the reward feels like punishment. (*Oh, ma, do I have to write today? I don't want to. I don't want to!* ... But you know that you really do want to, or you wouldn't be reading this book.)

Having said that, when you are writing all you have to be concerned about is this: What motivates the story? What motivates the story may be different with each story you write. And if what motivates your story to move forward—plot and character development, for instance—resonates with what motivates the reader to read, then bonus! You've written something that some people will want to read.

Speaking of motivation... As mentioned before, you might say a story without motivation is like a day without sunshine—a dull story, no matter what your personal motivation for writing. Such a story will motivate the reader to head for something like a cheese sandwich.

Story sparks

I want to separate what motivates you to write and what motivates the story to move forward—separate what sparks or inspires you to write a particular story from what sparks the plot and other elements of the story. For instance, in my short story, *The Conquest of Kong*, what you don't see is the inspiration behind it.

You don't see the author, a middle-aged man, occasionally reflecting on how he and his father never really connected. You don't see how that feeling of disconnectedness returns one day like a sudden storm when the man is on the midway of the Canadian National Exhibition (CNE). You don't see why it returns, why the trip to the CNE rekindles the childhood memory of the author and his father at a small fair where the father was enticed by the lure of a carney into playing a game that was almost impossible to win. You don't see the father winning several times. You don't see the carney calling him back to the game after each win, until the father, going after the bright prize, child at his side, loses.

What inspired the story was one thought that hit like a blinding flash as the author—yours truly—stood on the midway, surrounded, almost overwhelmed, by the sights and sounds and smells of the CNE:

What if I could have helped him win?

That was it. *What if?* That's what inspired the story—*what if?*—and inspires many stories.

It is *what if?* that lets the author create characters and plunk them down in time and space, and have them interact and relate with each other and secondary characters until the question is answered. But in creating this story, the author no longer exists. The "I" of the story is a character of my creation, but he is not me. He assumes a life and a quest of his own. And it his quest to find out *what if?* that motivates, or moves forward, the story. Yes, many of the emotions are mine, and some of the events are loosely based on things that happened, but the story is fiction. It has been pushed well beyond what occurred and didn't occur. In other words, my father/son psychobabble no longer matters, although it sparked the story idea. My lust for the drug of writing is immaterial, although it gets me writing. And whatever readers may or may not think of what I create is out of my control.

Without *what if?* I would not have pushed the truth, as I remember it, into the wonderful lies (or perhaps larger truths) of fiction.

If you are feeling blocked, asking *what if?* can help spark your writing. You don't have to ask it before you freefall or do any of the exercises in the book. But sometimes after you've done exercises in this book, you can look and see if the question has come up or if you can apply it to anything you've written. And that might inspire you to continue on with what you are writing. Looking for the answer to *what if?* (even if you ask the question after the fact) can help you find focus, which most stories needs to be effective.

In other words, later, in a more rational moment, after you have completed a writing gesture sketch or even a humble first draft, you can read it over and ask yourself: *Now what do I want to do with this?* The answer might be *nothing* or it might be *something.* If something, you might want to ask your internal editor to help you find the *what if?* to see if that sparks further writing and plot and character development, no matter what motivated you or sparked the writing in the first place.

Journal exercise

While you don't need a *what if?* to write, you might be intrigued by the *what if?* concept. If you are, take a moment and review some of the writing you have done. See if you can find a *what if* question underlining any of your writing. If you find it, write it out in full: *What if...?* (whatever the question seems to be). Use that question as the opening line in a directed freefall and see where your writing takes you.

Try to do this with at a couple of passages or see if you can come up with a couple of *what if* questions that inspire you to freefall.

When you have completed your *what if?* exercise, continue with the chapter.

What If? discovery

After writing the first draft of this chapter, I came across a passage on *what if?* by the novelist John Irving (*The World According to Garp, Cider House Rules, Hotel New Hampshire, The Fourth Hand* and other novels). It seems appropriate, so I've inserted here. John Irving writes:

> Janet [his wife] gave me the idea for *The Fourth Hand.* One night we were watching the news on television before we went to bed. A story about the nation's first hand transplant got our attention. There were only brief views of the surgical procedure, and hardly a word about how the patient—the recipient, as I thought of him—lost his hand in the first place. There was nothing about the donor. The new hand had to have come from someone who'd died recently; probably he'd had a family.
>
> Janet asked the inspiring question: "What if the donor's widow demands visitation rights with the hand?"
>
> Dr. John C. Baldwin, the Dean of Dartmouth Medical School, has assured me that this probably wouldn't happen in what we call real life—not without the unlikely concurrence of enough lawyers and medical ethicists to start a small liberal-arts college. But I always listen to the storytelling possibilities. Every novel I've written has begun with a "what if..."

Just as memories of childhood incidents can spur the imagination and inspire stories, so can almost any interesting *what if* question. In addition, the answers to such questions (in other words, the stories such questions inspire) can keep your reader reading by keeping them engaged in the quest to answer the question.

Can your *what if?* change?

Once you find inspiration, are you stuck with the triggering *what if*?

Not at all.

I know that the *what if* question that inspired *Last Summer at Barebones* (a novel I referred to earlier in the book) changed as the novelist worked on the book. In fact, the book started out as a short story inspired by: What if a young girl is expecting to have the best summer of her life and it turns into the worst summer of her life?

As Diane Baker Mason, the novelist, explored that concept in a short story, she found herself asking:

> What if a young girl is expecting to have the best summer of her life and it turns into the worst summer of her life, and the young girl blamed her older sister?

As she answered the question, she discovered/created a powerful antagonist with whom the young girl locked horns. But many words into what was becoming a novel, the *what if* question shifted, or expanded, yet again:

> What if a young girl expecting to have the best summer of her life has the worst summer of her life and blames her older sister, and the negative impact of that summer is so strong that ultimately the younger sister vows the most extreme revenge—murder?

If you were to read the opening of the novel, you might think that the *what if* question above was the first question asked. It wasn't. However, since that is what inspired the final story, it should come as no surprise that it shaped the novel. But if you read the novel analytically, you will see the evolution of the *what if* questions. But we are now into the academic claptrap that often spoils the read! So enough of that.

Now what?

If you have not already done so, look at some of what you have written. Try to find the inspiration for your writing, or see if what you have written can be used to inspire a *what if* question. If you don't see the *what if*, dig beneath the surface to find it. Ask yourself:

- What is my main character(s) trying to accomplish? Why?
- What/who stands in his/her way? Why?
- Will he overcome the obstacle(s)?
- If so, how and why? If not, why not?

The answers to these questions will help you shape your story, if you want to find and answer *what if?* and do more with something that you have written. But do not let this quest for inspiration interfere with the creative process. Seldom does it all come together in one shot.

My first drafts of *The Conquest of Kong* were miserable even though I was inspired and the story felt motivated. I had something I wanted and needed to say but was not saying it. It took me a while to understand the implications of the inspiration, before I could more clearly tell the story. But I did not let this lack of focus prevent me from creating. Without the initial work, I would have never discovered (and finished) the story I wanted to tell.

Journal exercise

Try to create *what if* scenarios of your own and see what kind of writing that inspires. Pose the *what if* question and flip into freefall. But if you need some help, pick any of these *what if* scenarios and use them as opening lines of directed freefalls:

- What if a character found a million dollars in a gym bag at the zoo?
- What if global warming destroyed life as we know it and left you living in a colony of 12 people?

- What if Sally and Diane attended a weeklong writers' conference and, to save money, shared a room with Peter, a writer with whom they were both secretly in love?
- What if you were on a plane that lost power and the captain said, "We have one minute before we hit that mountain up ahead..."? What would you write in the last minute of your life? (Use a timer and write for one minute only.)
- What if Stewart, a brilliant pianist (or artist or hockey player or something other) lost his left leg?
- What if Jillian was turned down for a promotion to VP of Marketing and discovered it was because of her gender (or ethnicity or sexual orientation, or the colour or her eyes)?
- What if your spouse divorced you and moved to the Cayman Islands, and only after your spouse moved, you discovered he or she had won $5 million in the lottery?
- What if you found a fly in your soup at an upscale restaurant?
- What if you came up with your own *what if*? and wrote something of interest to you?

Complete several *what if?* freefalls, then read on.

13 / Modelling to Write

Modelling overview

Westside Story. Love Story. Both works are modelled on Shakespeare's *Romeo and Juliet*, which was modelled on an older Italian play. In this chapter, you will make like Shakespeare and model your writing on works by other writers. The goal is not to copy works of others but to find inspiration through modelling. Why? Let's see what novelist Margaret Atwood has to say...

Word for thought

"*Read*," is what Margaret Atwood says when asked if she has any advice for neophyte writers.

But why read? I suggest Atwood means that you should read analytically—that you can learn how to write by analyzing how other writers have created their works and by analyzing the impact that other works have on you. Sometimes when you are struggling, stepping away from the writing and reading something for an hour or so can be a great way clear your head and overcome writer's block. And if it inspires you to model something you've read, bonus.

For instance, I tossed the book, *The Spy Who Came in from the Cold* (by John Le Carré) against the wall in anger when I got to the end. I was not angry with Le Carré; I was angry that a character I had come to know and feel for had died. It would make sense that, as a writer, I would get over my hissy-fit and re-read the book to analyze how Le Carré made me care about his fictional creation and to discover how he got such an emotional reaction out of me.

By the way, I would not expect you to react the same way to the novel: as readers, we reserve the right to react any way we please, or any way our emotions cause us to react. I cried at the end of the first chapter of *Shoeless Joe* by W. P. Kinsella. I knew I was in for a rough ride, but one that I was willing to go on. There is no guarantee that you would feel a thing. What was important, after my emotional reaction, was that I took a deep breath and read analytically—to learn from Kinsella.

If reading can help you become a better writer, then reading analytically can help even more. The next logical step then is to accelerate your learning by modelling other work.

When you model, you find inspiration in the work you are reading, and then you push it further—in any direction that makes sense to you based on your reaction to the work. I am not suggesting that you model the work of another writer and then rush out to find a publisher for your new creation. Modelling is simply an excellent way to inspire and sharpen your creative, analytical, writing and editing skills.

Having said that, let me point out again that Shakespeare's *Romeo and Juliet* was modelled on an older Italian play and that *Westside Story*, *Love Story* and *Romeo Must Die* (and other movies, plays and stories) were modelled on *Romeo and Juliet*. There is no denying the influence of the older works on the subsequent works, so developing a new twist on an old story can work. Many movies and TV shows are derivatives or spin-offs—derived from, spun off of or modelled on characters, plots and/or themes of other movies and TV shows. In most cases, this kind of modelling is done with credit given to the original work that inspired the derivative work. (But not always. Hey, that's showbiz!)

The goal here is to help you over come your block(s) by finding inspiration, developing characters, and creating events that ring true with you as writer (so they will ring true with readers). The emphasis is on creation, but modelling helps impose some sense of form or structure on your work and helps your creative side work in a more logical, linear manner. I'm not suggesting you should always create in a logical, linear manner; sometimes it doesn't hurt to do so. Always be open, but don't let your logical or linear side (your internal editor) block you by trying to impose form when you are exercising or warming up.

In the exercises below, my instructions are not dictates! Do whatever you feel comfortable with, but try to work on modelling the work presented, at least in your first pass. Now on with *modelling...*

Five modelling exercises

Modelling can include imitating the form or shape of a poem, the plot of a story, the theme or writing style or another piece of writing, copying the first line and letting it take you wherever (directed freefall), or simply finding inspiration in the work. In each of the exercises below, you will be given something to read followed by writing exercises that will help you model the original work in some way.

Exercise one

Short excerpt from *The Girl who Lived in a Shell*:

> Once upon a time, there was a little girl growing up in middle-class Toronto. She wore black patent leather shoes to church on Sunday, and watched her father sing in the choir. No one in her family argued on Sundays, they just "discussed" the sermon over roast beef and mashed potatoes. There was no alcohol in the house; they all drank ice water with meals....
> – Author unknown

Modelling instructions

What goes on around the dinner table can have a great impact on our lives, especially on the lives of children, particularly during meals that are served on religious holidays or festive occasions, or when company comes over.

The exercise here is meant to help you create a scene around dinner. You will use clustering, freefall and modelling to help you create your scene. You will take two passes at it—one using a line from the passage above and one using your own opening line so you can move away from the model and find your own voice and emotional centre, allowing you to create a scene that is yours.

Here is what I want you to do:

- Cluster the word *Dinner*.
- Once your cluster is complete, flip into a directed freefall, starting with "Once upon a time...."
- Once your freefall is finished, reread it. Look for a line in your freefall to use as the beginning of a new prose piece.
- Write down that line and try a new directed freefall...
- See where it takes you.

You don't have to do anything else with the freefalls, unless inspired to do something.

When you have completed the modelling exercise, continue with the chapter.

Exercise two

Excerpt from *President Cleveland Where Are You?* by Robert Cormier:

> That was the autumn of the cowboy cards—
> Buck Jones and Tom Tyler and Hoot Gibson and

especially Ken Maynard. The cards were available in those five-cent packages of gum: pink sticks, three together, covered with a sweet white powder. You couldn't blow bubbles with that particular gum, but it couldn't have mattered less. The cowboy cards were important—the pictures of those rock-faced men with eyes of blue steel.

On those wind-swept, leaf-tumbling afternoons we gathered after school on the sidewalk in front of Lemur's Drugstore, across from St. Jude's Parochial School, and we swapped and bargained and matched for the cards.

Because a Ken Maynard serial was playing at the Globe every Saturday afternoon, he was the most popular cowboy of all, one of his cards was worth at least ten of any other kind. Rollie Tremaine had a treasure of thirty or so, and he guarded them jealously. He'd match you for the other cards, but he risked his Ken Maynards only when the other kids threatened to leave him out of the competition altogether...

Modelling instructions

This excerpt evokes many 'things'. I am being vague here because I want you to make a list of the 'things' it evokes for you—your personal equivalents. For instance, I'd substitute 'winter' for 'autumn' and 'hockey cards' for 'baseball cards'; you might substitute 'summer' and 'sea shells'.... *Whatever.*

- Pick your season(s) and your thing(s) and jot them down; once your list is complete, reread the passage.
- Go back to an equivalent time and place in your life and freefall. (If it helps get you started, model the opening line—"That was the autumn of the cowboy cards..." Only substitute your season and thing, and freefall.... See where it takes you.)

Again, you don't have to do anything else with the freefall, unless inspired to do something.

When you have completed your second modelling exercise, continue with the chapter.

Exercise three

Read the short poem by Al Purdy below, and then follow the instructions.

She wears glasses
and has a slightly
intellectual look
as if she were about
to read a book,
and then decided
against it

Modelling instructions

After reading the poem, think of somebody you know and focus on one aspect of that person. The aspect could be an article of clothing, hat, gesture, walk, hairstyle, mannerism, way of speaking, etc.

Once you've focused on the person and the particular aspect, write down all the things it might represent (just as glasses are often used to represent intellectualism).

Then write down the opposites of what it might represent.

Now try to model the seven-line poem above. Use it as a template to help you shape your poem. It can be difficult trying to force form on content, but I want you to try this for several people that you can think of.

If you are feeling inspired, once you have tried the above exercise, write a longer poem about one person. Play with it. Play with form, style, rhyme (or lack thereof). Play with expectations, and dashed expectations.... See where it all takes you.

Or...

Model the first line (based on the gender of the person you are thinking of, and the 'aspect' of the person), and freefall.... There is no wrong way to do this, as long as you write! Again, see where it takes you. Once you arrive, move on to the next exercise.

When you have completed your third modelling exercise, continue with the chapter.

Exercise four

Read the poem below, by Tamar S. (a Toronto high school student) then follow the modelling instructions.

I was with my dad
When I was two
He was painting
I think I was two
He left the room
For a minute
BIG MISTAKE
When he came back
He almost fainted
The room was painted purple and red
And I had a multi-coloured head
But he was proud of me
He still calls me an artist

Modelling instructions

- Pick a parent (or guardian or other relative). Jot down his or her name and relationship to you.
- Pick a time (you at a particular age) when that person was around.
- Pick an event—something that happened during the time you have picked.
- Pick a consequence—spell it out.
- Pick a name that your parent (guardian or relative) calls you or would have called you if the event had inspired a nickname.
- Now... Model the poem as exactly as you can. Use the same number of lines and line length.... Notice the judicious use of rhyme (fainted, painted; red, head) and the effect it has. Try to model the rhyme as well and the use of CAPITALS.

This might feel like tough work—work that puts your editor and creator in conflict. Your creator might want to ride the wind, meanwhile your editor is saying: "Hold on. This line is too long. The rhyme goes here, not there." That's okay. Let them fight. Or work together. See what you come up with because part of what you need to learn is how and when to work with your editor. So go at it. *Try it before you read on.*

And then...

Once you have slavishly adhered to the form and completed your poem, try a second version. Go through the same "pick" process you did above. Find someone new or use one of your above "picks."

Then use the opening line of the poem—"I was with my... [whomever] when I was [whatever age]"—to start a directed freefall. Run with it. Freefall a long prose passage and see what you create.

And then...

Use the nickname as a key word, cluster it. Flip into freefall when you have completed your clustering.

Many options, I know. You can do it all in one sitting, or over several sittings. Either way, the goal here is to write! To find some inner emotion that ends up inspiring your writing.

When you have completed your fourth modelling exercise, continue with the chapter.

Exercise five

Read the William Carlos Williams poem below and then follow the modelling instructions.

This Is Just To Say

I have eaten
the plums
that were in
the icebox
and which
you were probably
saving
for breakfast
Forgive me
they were delicious
so sweet
and so cold

Modelling instructions

Think of something you've done that a nagging voice in the back of your mind occasionally (or frequently) reminds you of and tells you to apologize for. Ideally, this is something you have not apologized for. Mind you, if you are Canadian, you have apologized for everything you have done. I once bumped into a telephone pole and said, "Sorry." But I digress....

Once you've focused on the event and the people involved, freefall a letter. To help you, divide your freefall letter into three distinct sections:

- Describe what you did
- Describe why you did it
- Apologise for doing it

If it helps, start your freefall with "Dear (name)"—the name of the person you are apologizing to. Once you have written the three-part freefall letter, read on.

When you have completed the first part of your fifth modelling exercise, continue with the chapter.

Now...

A letter has one point of view (POV)—from that of the writer. With that in mind, what I want you to do now is this: Flip your freefall around. Answer the freefall letter with another freefall letter written in the voice of the person you have apologized to....

In other words, take the other person's POV and reply. If you want a directed freefall line, try this:

I have read what you have to say and....

After your second freefall, you may want your first character to reply. And then have your second character reply again.... Your call. Have fun and, as always, see where it takes you.

When you have completed the second part of your fifth modelling exercise, continue with the chapter.

Flipping POV

Why did I have you flip POV? You may already have some sense of the answer. Short stories, novels—even feature non-fiction articles—look at relationships, incidents, subject matter, and so on from multiple points of view, even though there tends to be one dominant character. You need to be able to see whatever it is you are writing from the perspective of more than one character.

Yes, you will have a main POV. You might even create a character who is blind to the points of view of all other characters in the story. But there will be others, and they will have to interact with your main character. So there will more than one take on issues or more than one POV, even if your main character cannot see beyond the end of his or her nose.

With that in mind, go back over the work you have created in the modelling chapter, or in any other chapter, and see if you can introduce other points of view into anything.

If you have a freefall that has an exceptionally focused POV, write it from the perspective of another character. For instance, look at your journey through childhood exercises. Are they all written from the POV of you as a child (or from the POV of the fictional children you created)? Absolutely fine if they are. However, now is your opportunity to rewrite them from the POV of a sibling, parent or guardian, other adult, or other child. Or perhaps you can rewrite a passage keeping your POV but introducing the POV of another character who gets to interact with your first character.

Seeing the same situation or events from multiple points of view will make you a more mature writer and it will help you expand what may seem like short passages into longer, more complex writing. In other words, play with POV. And have some fun doing it.

This is a great writing exercise to do when you are feeling blocked. Sometimes looking at a situation from the perspective of another character, or simply finding another point of view, can help open up the floodgates and get you writing. Doesn't mean you have to use what you write, but it can get you writing, and then, when you come back to your work from your original point of view, you suddenly discover you do have something to write about.

This method can be used in writing non-fiction too. Do you want to write a stirring speech in favour or opposed to some issue? Are you having difficulty getting started? Take the opposing point of view. If you are in favour of something, write as if you oppose it, or vice versa. This helps you see the other side of the issue, even if you don't particularly want to see it, and it can help you produce a sounder, rounder and more reasoned argument when you return to your point of view.

Other modelling exercises

Here are some other modelling exercises you can try. See where they take you:

- Pick other poems to model
- Model the opening paragraphs of other short stories or novels
- Model a poem, but then turn your model into prose
- Model a letter to the editor, an editorial, newspaper column or article
- Model a Hallmark card
- Model the opposite of a Hallmark card; turn the sentiment on its head in a prose passage

Read. Read analytically. Learn from what you like, and from what does not appeal to you. Use modelling to apply what you learn and see where it takes you.

Try a final modelling exercise or try a second POV exercise before you read on.

14 / Look Who's Talking

My short story, *The Conquest of Kong*, is a first person narrative. It's told in first person, from the point of view of the son. The reader sees and knows only what the son sees and knows.

> It was on the congested grounds of the Canadian National Exhibition that Father conquered the world-famous ape. The glassy-eyed creature, wearing a New York Yankee baseball cap, glared down at the midway masses from his perch in the Strike Out tent. I sometimes wonder how we must have appeared from Kong's vantage point—my brawny father with premature flecks of grey dotting slicked-back waves and his scrawny kid with the bristled brush cut.

While it could have been told in first person from the POV of the Father, it would have been a different story. If a story is told in first person, all the events that make up the story must come from the narrator (the person narrating or telling the story, not the person writing it—unless you want to include authorial intrusions like Charles Dickens often did).

The story could have also been told in third person by an omnipotent narrator (not a person in the story; more like an external story-telling voice) but I felt that third person would have inhibited the intimacy that I was trying to achieve between my characters. Achieving this intimacy was not a conscious part of the freefall, but discovering it and maintaining it through the use of first person was a conscious act of my internal editor.

A third person narrator can be omnipotent (all seeing) or limited. Like God, an omnipotent narrator knows everything each character is thinking and can present the story from the perspective of multiple characters. This form is more often used in novels (rather than short stories) with complex plots and large casts of characters like historical works that cover generations. Limited third person can be effectively used in short stories and novels. A limited third person narrator only knows what one character knows or sees. In other words, the narrator stays out of the heads of other characters. However, the thoughts/actions of other characters can be revealed through the protagonist once the protagonist discovers what another character is thinking or doing.

Imagine a mystery novel unfolding:

> Johnson woke up in his worn black leather chair that was tucked in close to his cluttered office desk. He heard a thumping noise, lifted his head off his day planner, and realised the noise was coming from inside his head. He groaned, sat up and straightened his rumpled jacket sleeves. That's when it dawned on him: he was still wearing the suit he had worn to Mallory's Bar last night. It looked much worse for his having slept in it, and he was very hung over. Again.
>
> He could remember little of what had transpired during the previous evening beyond entering Mallory's Bar, meeting a gorgeous blonde—had Mallory introduced them or had she just appeared by his side?—and buying her a drink. After that? Things were foggier than a rain forest mist.

She must have slipped something into my drink, he thought. Just as that thought entered his mind, he noticed a blood stain, very red and very dry, on his shirt cuff. Before he could investigate it, a thump roused him. This one came from the office door, not his head. He pulled the arms of his jacket down and covered the stain.

"Yeah?" he called. "Door's open."

In walked the blonde. All six-feet two inches of her statuesque beauty. Johnson gulped.

"Tough night after I left?" she asked, moving close to him.

"Tell me about it."

"I take it you'd like to know."

"I've got the big picture," he said, not wanting to tip his hand. "But there are a few details I'm a bit foggy on."

She laughed. "Foggy is exactly how you look."

"But I can see you clearly enough. So tell me this—if we were at the same place at the same time last night, why do I feel as if I've been run over by a dump truck, and why do you look like you've just stepped off the cover of Vogue?"

As the blonde sat at the edge of his desk and leaned in close, Johnson was concerned she might see the blood on his sleeve. He had to think fast—get her out of his office and get changed, without losing sight of her...

This is limited third person. Readers know what Johnson is thinking and how he feels, but they don't know anything about 'the blonde'—not even her name. Nor will the reader know anything about her unless Johnson finds out. So while the story is told in the third person, the POV is limited to whatever Johnson knows, sees, hears or otherwise discovers.

Wow, was that an information dump or what? Does your brain hurt? Or was it all old hat? So why did I tell you this, you may be wondering. Sometimes, when one is blocked, the problem is not a lack of ideas or a lack of plot. The problem is, or can be, the narrative voice.

While there really is no right or wrong voice, there can be a right or wrong voice for telling a particular story. Sometimes the block occurs because the writer is using the wrong voice *for the story*. There is only one way to find out if that is what is blocking you. Change voice.

"But I've written 100 pages in first person!" you protest.

Yes, and you are now blocked. Just because you have written it in first person does not mean you are using the right voice for the story. The only way you will find out is to experiment. The 100 pages you've written won't go away while you play with voice. Which leads us to...

... Journal exercises

By now you should have accumulated a small body of work based on your freefalls, clustering, journeys through childhood and modelling.

If you look at your work, you may notice that some of what you have written is in first person and some in third. Pick something that you've written in first person and rewrite it in third person to see how it feels and what impact it has on the story.

And after that, pick something that you've written in third person and rewrite it in first person to see how it feels and what impact it has on the story.

Conversely, if you've been working on something in particular and have hit a wall, take a look at the voice you've been using, and change your voice to see if that new take on an old story helps you move it forward.

The goal here, beyond the writing exercise, is for you to see what impact using first and third person can have on the tone and style of your work and to see if a fresh perspective, at least in terms of voice, can get you writing.

Try at least two voice exercises before you read on.

15 / Characters of Fiction

There are many elements of fiction: plot, setting, voice (as we've discussed) and character development, all come to mind. And there are many books out there that go into great detail on the elements of fiction. I'd like to spend a bit of time on one aspect: characters. Sometimes blocks occur because a writer does not know his or her characters well enough; they don't come alive for the writer. If you know your characters well, they can almost take on a life of their own. And some writers would suggest that I strike the 'almost' in that sentence. Or as one writer put it: "My characters are telling their story. I'm just the vehicle to convey it from the characters to the page." For that to happen, you have to know your characters intimately.

Characters are the people (animals, creatures, avatars) that populate your fiction. All stories contain major characters (generally a protagonist and an antagonist) and most contain a supporting cast of minor characters. Through dialogue or action that has an impact on a major character, a minor character can serve a particular function.

In the following example, a minor character serves a function without doing anything:

> Outside the subway station, I caught the Bay bus heading south, heading towards divorce court. Divorce court. Divorce. Who would have thunk it possible. Not I, not 20 years ago when Lydia and I took our vows. Twenty years ago, wedded bliss. And now I am on my way to divorce court—all due to her.

> I was totally wrapped up in my thoughts—my divorce court defence strategies—when I handed the bus driver my transfer. But when the driver said "thank you" her voice jolted me out of my reverie.
>
> Good-gawd, I thought. A woman driver. Figures. Here I am unemployed with a wife about to take me to the cleaners over child support and alimony payments I can ill afford and there is a dame driving this rig. She probably has a husband making a mint as a bank executive and her salary is paying for their time-share vacation condo in Hawaii.
>
> "You're welcome," I muttered and moved to the back of the bus...

Simply by existing, the minor character has served a function. She started an internal monologue in the main character that helps reveal a great deal about the character's attitude towards women. No doubt, his attitude will come into play as the story progresses.

The major characters, as I've said, include a protagonist or hero, (who tends to dominate the action) and the antagonist or opponent (the one who acts against, opposes or butts heads with the protagonist). Yes, you can have two or more people working together as protagonists, although one usually is seen as the main character. And you can have a team of antagonists. Again, one usually dominates. (Or you could even have one character climbing a mountain, trying to reach the peak. The climber could be your protagonist and the mountain could be the antagonist.)

You do not want stories, particularly short stories, to be overly cluttered with characters. Some fiction, however, has a cast of hundreds. In historical novels that span centuries, heroes and antagonists change from generation to generation (unless there is a vampire or poltergeist that spans generations). Episodic stories might involve a hero interacting with (fighting and defeating) a series of antagonists. For instance, punished by the gods for killing his family (in a fit of insanity inflicted upon him by one of the gods), Hercules has to perform 12 labours—feats so difficult that they seem impossible—each against a different antagonist.

Character types

There are several types of characters. A flat character is known by one or two character traits. A round character is complex and multi-dimensional. A stock character is a stereotyped character (mad scientist, absent-minded professor). Static characters remain the same from beginning to end. Dynamic characters undergo change. Change must be within the realm of possibility; the character must be motivated and allowed sufficient time to change. Character types used should be appropriate to the genre (romance, mystery, crime, sci-fi, spy, literary) and type (comedy, drama) of story as well as the plot.

Character differentiation

So that your characters don't all look alike, sound alike and act alike, characters should have distinct features. It is particularly important for you to know your main characters well—to have a solid sense of who they are. Yes, there can be similarities between two major characters, but differences are required. Not all of the character traits you create for your characters will enter into your story, but it doesn't hurt to be aware of the need to differentiate your characters and to create a list of differences on the side. Sometimes you can determine all this before your write; other times these character aspects evolve as you write.

Differences often become apparent as the characters come into conflict, attempt to resolve conflicts and move forward on their journey. These differences help the reader keep the characters separate in their minds. The differences also allow the reader to become engaged with characters as individuals or to feel conflicted over which character(s) to invest emotional energy in. If the reader cannot invest emotional energy in your characters, they will abandon your story.

Have characters started to raise their heads in your writing? Are you interested in any of the characters populating any of your work? Do you have at least two characters in any of your work that you would like to develop? If so, pick two and use the character sketch list below to put flesh on their bones. Get down as much detail as possible. Then go back to whatever you are working on that includes the characters you sketch out here, and start writing again. Or use the journal exercise below to try to further develop your characters.

Character inventory exercise

Pick at least two characters you have met through your writing so far, or that you are developing in anything else you are writing, and fill in the blanks in the chart below. Get to know your characters as intimately as possible before you put them into scenarios and have them interact.

<table>
<tr>
<td>
• Name:
• Gender:
• Date of Birth:
• Born in: city/state:
• Zodiac sign:

• Father's Name (and age):
• Mother's Name (and age):
• Siblings' Names/Ages):
• List of important relatives:
• Serious friends then and
</td>
<td>
• Political orientation at various ages:
• Social causes, if any:
• Recycler: Yes or No

• Phobias:
• Hobbies / Interests:
• Passion(s):
• Believes in: aliens / God / reincarnation / after life / heaven / hell / the bible
</td>
</tr>
</table>

now (names, gender, when they met, first impressions where are they now)...

- Friends...

...up to age 5:
...5 to 12:
...12 to 16:
...16 to 21:
...21 and on

- Height/weight of your main characters at each age above:
- Hair colour/style at each age:
- Colour of eyes:
- Complexion:
- Body shape/size:

- Bed wetter: (If yes, until age)
- Favourite toys:
- Major illnesses:
- Bones broken:
- List of serious and/or memorable accidents:

- Pet Peeves:
- Favourite Colour:
- Least Fav. Colour:
- Favourite Food:
- Least Fav. Food:
- Fav. Dessert:
- Fav. Junk Food:

- Education: (programs, courses, locations of institutions, degrees / diplomas / certificates)
- Work Experience: (companies, positions, dates from/to)

- Current Marital Status:
- Previous Marital Statuses:
- Sexual Orientation: (hetero, homo, bi-sexual, bi-curious)

- First memory (details):
- Repressed memories: (details):
- First Kiss: (when, with who, how did it happen)
- First base: (when, with who, how did it happen)
- Second Base: (when, with who, how did it happen)
- Third Base: (when, with who, how did it happen)
- Virgin or not:
- Lost virginity - age, to whom, how:
- Most recent sexual experience:
- Fav. sexual experience:
- Worst sexual experience:
- Orgasm: yes / no / how...)

• Vegetarian or carnivore • Fav. Movie: • Fav. Song: • Fav. Group/Singer: • Fav. TV shows through the ages: • Fashion sense (describe): • Fav. Clothes • EST moments... ...happiest when: ...saddest when: ...depressed when: ...angriest when: ...most bored when: ...most agitated when: ...most frightened when: ...calmest when: ...funniest when: • Travel: (where, when): • Sports: watches / plays:	• Manner in which he/she talks • Attitude towards own physical appearance • Attitudes towards the opposite sex, others in society, family and friends • Fighting manner: flight or fight • Conflict resolution (or lack thereof) manner • Dreams: yes / no • Recurring dream(s): • Sleep patterns: • Morning or evening person: • Dink of choice: coffee/tea; alcohol • Other personality traits:

Journal exercise

Enough character sketching. Let's do some writing!

Pick two characters you have created, or feel free to create a couple of new characters. Create character inventories based on the character differentiation features above. Feel free to add relevant categories.

Once you have an inventory of your characters completed, place your characters in the scenario below and have them interact. You will not use all inventory attributes in the scenario, and you may even discover things you didn't know about your characters. The point is to get to know your characters well, and in knowing them, make them credible and interesting when they appear in your writing.

The scenario

Your characters are the only two people in an elevator when the power goes out. The elevator is stuck for about 20 minutes. What do they do, how do they react, what do they say (or not say) to each other?

Feeling claustrophobic? Use the elevator scenario to see where your characters take you. Then feel free to put them into different situations to see how they react and evolve.

Put two characters in an elevator and have them interact for about 20 minutes before you read on.

Other scenarios

Put the same characters, or two other characters, in other scenarios. For instance, you can have them stranded on the top of a mountain. (How did they get there? Is it important? Did they arrive together or separately?) Or have them meet in a bar. Or perhaps they are working out beside each other at the gym. Or put them in bed together. Or have them be stranded on the moon... Again, what do they say? How do they react and interact?

Put two characters in different scenarios and have them interact for about 20 minutes before you read on.

Don't stop there

Speaking of "what they say", put your characters in the scenario of your choice and have them talk with no narrative interruption. Use dashes to distinguish changes in vocabulary, but don't use any "he said" or "she said" and don't describe them in any way or describe where they are or any actions they might take. Simply let everything unfold through dialogue. See if you can differentiate the two characters based on dialogue only.

Take the elevator scenario. It might go something like this:

- Oh God, I don't believe it. I hope it's only temporary. I've got to get to the ninth floor by noon.
- I ride these elevators every day; this always happens.
- Your kidding? It happens every day?
- No, but often... It never lasts more than a minute. I can see by my Blackberry that it's 11:55. You should be fine.
- Can you put that in writing for me?
- No, but I can email it to you...

Put two characters in a scenario have them interact before you read on.

Don't stop there

Try your characters in scenes that make sense, based on who they are. Keep the scenario to two characters; work on creating two distinct characters—each with their own voice and their own quirks. See if you can take two characters through a situation to a climactic moment.

Have fun sketching your characters and then putting them into various scenarios, including ones that make sense and ones that may not make sense. The work you do here will pay off when you have real characters coming into conflict in real situations.

When you have completed at least one other character differentiation exercises, read on.

16 / Show Versus Tell

Almost every writing student has heard this rule: Show, don't tell. It's a solid rule, but the principle can be difficult to master.

Telling is the reliance on simple exposition:

> Mary was an old woman.

Showing, on the other hand, uses evocative description:

> Mary moved slowly across the room, her hunched form supported by a polished wooden cane gripped in a gnarled, swollen hand that was covered by liver-spotted skin.

Showing and telling as used above convey the same information—Mary is old. Telling states it flat-out. And showing? Read the example over and you will see it never states that Mary is old, yet leaves no doubt about it. Now compare the two passages below.

Passage one

> My father was cruel man. When I was a child, he often hurt me and caused me great pain. One day he beat me simply because I was crying.

Passage two

> The day I turned five I cried uncontrollably for some reason. I can't really recall why.

> My father was deeply ensconced in the couch cushions, watching a football game and drinking beer. "Shut your friggin' yap, for christsake!" he shouted.
>
> Maybe I was hungry; we had so little food then. Maybe I was sad because my mother had been in bed all day, again. I continued to bellow. A second time my father shouted at me, but I cried on—an inconsolable prisoner in rickety, splintered wooden playpen prison.
>
> A third time: "If you don't stop, right now," he said, and paused to take a deep swig of beer, "I will give you something to cry about."
>
> I did not stop. I could not stop.
>
> My father did not tell me a fourth time.
>
> He turned and threw the half-empty beer bottle at me, hitting me flush in the temple and silencing me until long after the ambulance arrived and took me to the hospital...

In the second passage, I do not use the words "pain" or "hurt" or "cruel." But you see all of that and more. I suspect your reaction to the second passage is stronger that your reaction to the first because I am showing you what went on.

Showing helps the reader see your images rather than filling in the blanks with images of their own. When reviewers use terms like "vivid," "evocative" or "cinematic" to describe a novel, they mean the writer has succeeded at showing, rather than merely telling.

Apply show versus tell

First off, do not let this concept interfere with your creation. I tend to tell more than show in my first drafts. I don't want to get bogged down in the details of show. But I know some marvellous writers who can effortlessly paint word pictures in a first draft. If you feel you lack show details in your writing, you can look for opportunities to add them later. This is where the editor and creator work hand in hand.

The editor finds the opportunities and then hands them off to the creator who expands a passage or writes a new one. In other words, as you read your work over, look for opportunities to show. You don't have to show everything, but if you want to engage your reader and if you want your reader to see what you are writing, you have to show or create word pictures for the reader.

Do you remember *The Nuncles*?

The details in that story were layered on over several drafts as my creator and editor worked hand in hand. If that is what it takes to get where you want to go, then that is what it takes. Not understanding that there is a process to this can block writers. You write, you read it. You think it isn't good enough. You quit. I suggest that after you write, read and have your little pout over it not being stellar writing, you take a deep breath, go for a walk, and then return to the writing and work on it.

(On the other hand, if you are able to show as your freefall, don't pull back, even if you think you've gone over the top. Just as the editor can help you add detail, the editor can help you cut back too.)

Journal exercises

With show versus tell in mind, edit a freefall (or several freefalls). Look for opportunities to show rather than tell a couple of traits for each character, setting, situation or attitude in the work.

1. Pick one of your characters from your character differentiation work, and show him or her. Paint as vivid a portrait as possible of this person—age, body type, and personality, without using concrete words like "old" or "fat" or "dull".

2. Pick one of your journey through childhood or modelling exercises and rewrite it with show in mind. Look for opportunities to add details that will make the reader see what you see in your mind's eye.
3. Remember our mad, sad, scared, glad exercise from way back when? Pick one of the scenarios that you created for one of the emotions. Revise it with "show" in mind. Make sure you show the emotions you (or any of your characters) were feeling, without using any words that state any emotions that were felt.
4. Leave your computer behind. Take your writer's journal outside. Find a bench and gesture sketch all that you can see.
    a. If a car speeds by, don't tell us it was speeding. Show us.
    b. If you are in a park and can hear squirrels chattering, don't tell us they are chattering. Make us hear them.
    c. If you are in a café and the waiter is rude, don't tell us he (or she) was rude. Show us. And if the waiter is gorgeous or handsome, don't tell us, show us! Make us see what you see. And in that way we will feel what you feel as well

When you have completed a couple of show versus tell exercises, please read on.

17 / Critiquing and Editing

This is not a book on editing your work to produce a final, polished version. But I've included a couple of thoughts on editing for your consideration.

Rome wasn't built in a day. Few, if any, complete works of literature are either. Work should be edited. Problems often occur when we try to edit as we are trying to create. Many of us have suppressed our spontaneous, child-like creative self for so long that we can't create without criticizing what we write and trying to improve it as we write. I'd suggest to you that that is an ineffective use of invoking your editor.

Your editor is like that grade five teacher we knew and loathed—okay, that I knew and loathed. But you probably have an equivalent teacher. Mine was the critic who made me write with a pencil when all the other kids in the class were using pens. Why did I have to use a pencil? Because my O's weren't round enough, I crossed my t's too high and my a's looked like e's. And I couldn't spell worth a darn... That's who I equate my internal editor/critic with. Or should I say, "That's with whom I equate my internal editor"?

You see, my internal editor constantly squawks: "Don't end sentences with prepositions! Brawwwk!" Well, guess what? If it feels right, I end sentences with prepositions and cheerfully ignore my internal editor as he squawks away impotently. But you have to recognize your internal editor before you can overcome him or her, and then start to work constructively with you editor. With that in mind...

...Journal exercise

Do you have an internal critic/editor analogy? If one springs to mind, write about him/her/it. Write a freefall that starts with:

My internal editor reminds me of....

Go. Do it. Have fun. Then we'll look at some editing information.

When you have completed your internal editor freefall, continue with the chapter.

Editing can be daunting

Revising and editing can be daunting, intimidating even. However, it is an important part of the writing process—in its place. When editing, there's so much to look for—pacing, characterization, plot, theme, style, and so on—that a writer can get lost. When you sit down to write the first draft of a chapter or story, the jumble of clumsy words appearing on the screen is far from the perfect passages you'd imagined would come out. Experienced writers know that the jumble is not a problem because they realize that the more they revise the jumble, the closer they can bring it to their imagined state of perfection.

The early drafts lay down the foundation—the basic plot and characters; the final drafts fine-tunes what is there—building on the foundation and sometimes even rebuilding it. Early drafts are part of the discovery process, when the writing is most liquid. At this stage you are free to add or delete passages, go in a different direction than intended, play with characters and so on. You are more daring because the story is still uncharted. But once you have charted it—have the characters you want, doing and saying the things you want, in the order you want—you are ready to work on the final draft, or at least what feels like your final draft, before you start getting feedback from others on your work.

Editing: before and after

Let's look at a passage before and after editing takes place.

Before

> When promulgating your esoteric cogitations and articulating your philosophical observations beware of platitudinous ponderosity, and let your conversational communications possess a clarified conciseness and a compact comprehensibleness without coalescent consistency or a concatenated cogency. Eschew all conglomerations of flatulent garrulity, jejune babblement and asinine affectations and let your extemporaneous descantings have a voracious vivacity without rodomontade sagacity.

After

> Speak briefly, say what you mean, mean what you say and, above all, don't use big words.

Sometimes the need for a thorough edit is fairly evident, no?

While the before passage looks like it came straight out of a Dilbert cartoon, you'd be amazed at the extent to which some internal corporate communications is virtually unintelligible due to the utilization (use) of gargantuan (big) words where perfectly fine diminutive (small) ones will do. When writing, try to avoid jargon. Jargon and the use of colossal (big) words usually stems from an attempt to impress readers, but generally has the opposite effect.

Having said that, I love the sound of the words *gargantuan* and *colossal*, whereas *big* can sound dull, uninspired, unimaginative, bland...So the best advice I can give you is this: use words that are appropriate to the subject matter and audience. Also, make sure the words coming out of the mouths of your characters make sense, based on who the characters are and how they would communicate.

Speaking of Dilbert, here's an example of jargon from *The Dilbert Principle*, a book by Dilbert creator, Scott Adams: "I utilized a multi-tined implement to process a starch resource."

Translation: "I used my fork to eat a potato."

Again, sometimes the need for an edit is fairly evident, no?

Five editor chores

Your internal editor has several basic chores:

1. To help your creator put flesh on the bones of your idea
2. To make sure the story—plot, characters, setting, narrative structure, tone and writing style—work together (in fiction)
3. To make sure the most suitable words and phrases are used
4. To ensure the writing sounds as potent or lyrical as it should (particularly in poetry)
5. To ensure the writing is technically accurate.

It takes work, a combination of thought and experimentation, to edit effectively because, when writing, the possibilities seem endless. Editing comes quite naturally to some; others would rather sit in a tub full of worms than edit. Either way, editing is part of the process. If you have difficulty editing, consider taking a night school or online editing courses or hiring an editor to help you with your final draft. The fact is, most published authors have editors. (I've had two editors look at this book, and probably could have used a third!)

So work with your editor, but at the right time, to decide if you want to pursue a specific idea or turn a journal entry into a draft. Do this after you've completed a rough draft so you can take it to the next level, or after you've taken it to the next level, or after you've workshopped a story and received constructive feedback on it.

18 / Leading Up to Something

Leads are important. They draw the reader into your work and set the tone for all that follows. Many book buyers read the first few paragraphs or pages of a book and buy (or do not buy) based on the lead.

Take a moment and read the three leads below (one of which you have already read) before you read why they are here.

From Tom Clancy's *Shadow Watch*

> Later, when it became both her job and obsession to determine what happened at the pad, she would remember how everything had gone just right until it all went terribly wrong, turning excitement and anticipation into horror, and forever changing the course of her life. Astronaut, media celebrity, role model, mother—the world's easy reference tags for her would remain the same. But she knew herself well. There was the Annie Caulfield who had existed before the disaster, and the Annie Caulfield who eventually arose from its ashes. They were two very different women.

From Diane Baker Mason's *Last Summer at Barebones*

I go back to Barebones Lake the Wednesday before the Saturday on which I plan to shoot my sister.

The road lopes through the woods, there only by the grace of the forest's indulgence, and the car rides it bareback, spitting gravel from its tires at the turns. At the wheel of the car is me, instead of the Dad, and it's a sporty Mazda instead of a cumbersome, fishtailing Vistacruiser wagon. My Mazda has a CD player, and a LED digital display for its gauges, the wagon had dials with pointed needles that glowed phosphorescent in the dusk, and a pushbutton radio which, north of Severn River, only brought in static.

It's thirty years since I spent those seven summers on the island. The last was the summer before I turned fourteen....

Ffrom *The Conquest of Kong*

It was on the congested grounds of the Canadian National Exhibition that Father conquered the world-famous ape. The glassy-eyed creature, wearing a New York Yankee baseball cap, glared down at the midway masses from his perch in the Strike Out tent. I sometimes wonder how we must have appeared from Kong's vantage point—my brawny father with premature flecks of grey dotting slicked-back waves and his scrawny kid with the bristled brush cut.

Above the crowd the titanic brute, the most coveted prize at the CNE, seemed unconquerable.

Now what?

What did you think? Did you notice any similarities between the three leads? If not, go back and read them again. Read *analytically*.

What do you find out in each lead?

I won't keep you in suspense... for too long.

First, let me say, they are all about completely different topics, subjects and people. No doubt about that. If you were at all intrigued by the lead of *Shadow Watch*, I'm sorry to say that the rest of the novel is a major disappointment. But what a lead! "Later." What a great first word. To start a novel with what happens *later*? And what impact what happens later will have on Annie?

Last Summer at Barebones lives up to the expectations it creates. The question is: Were you hooked by the lead? Do you think she kills her sister? The only way you are going to find out is by reading the book, no?

You've already heard about *The Conquest of Kong.* Now analyse the story's lead. What does the title tell you? What does the first paragraph tell you? Is the father going to conquer Kong?

Do you see where I am going with this?

None of these leads could have been written without the author knowing what was going to happen "later...."

The first word of the Clancy's novel is not "Now" or "Previously" but a word that alludes to the future. As reader, you know from the first line that something happened and that it is going to *change* (delta factor) "Annie Caulfield who had existed before the disaster, and the Annie Caulfield who eventually arose from its ashes." You already know that the two Annies "were two very different women" and that a disaster is going to occur.

The question is: Do you want to go for the journey to see how and why Annie changes? That is the question, I put to you, the question that all readers ask: *Do I want to go on the journey to see if anything happens*?

Before an author can start a novel or short story with a lead that foreshadows the outcome, the author has gone on the journey. The first several drafts are the author's journey alone. If you do not finish the first draft and get to some place called "the end" how are you ever going to start your story? You have to know your destination before you can figure out where to start so you can plot a route to get you from beginning to end.

Look at Mason's opening again: "I go back to Barebones Lake the Wednesday before the Saturday on which I plan to shoot my sister." Mason has to know what is going to happen to write a lead like that. Do you want to go on the journey and find out if the main character does what she plans to do?

Look at the transition sentence, the sentence that takes you out of the lead and into the story: "It's thirty years since I spent those seven summers on the island. The last was the summer before I turned fourteen...." The journey begins there. We will find out what happened that summer; no doubt it will tell us why she plans to kill her sister.

As Mason told me in an interview: "I had no idea what was going to happen when I started this novel. It wasn't until I found out what was going to happen, that I could come back and write the beginning of the novel." Once she reached her destination, she could go back and begin her journey. Yes, she had to start somewhere in her first draft before she could reach her destination. But that does not mean she could not go back and revisit/revise her beginning once she reached her destination.

Again, let us look at *The Conquest of Kong*:

> It was on the congested grounds of the Canadian National Exhibition that Father conquered the world-famous ape.

Sentence one tells us that Father conquers Kong, does it not? So why bother with this: "Above the crowd the titanic brute, the most coveted prize at the CNE, seemed unconquerable." We know Kong can be conquered. The question is: *Do you want to go on the journey to see how Father conquered something that seemed unconquerable*? It is as simple as that. However, and I suspect you know this already, the story is about more Father conquering Kong, is it not? It is about a boy and his father developing a bond that, the reader learns, was not there at the beginning. It is about change. Just as Mason's story will be about more than one sister shooting or not shooting another. There will be change.

Clancy's story should have been about Annie changing. In fact, it is about a whole lot that does not relate to Annie at all. The novel loses focus or a sense of purpose and falls flat, or does not pay off. But still, what a brilliant lead!

Find Endings

The exercises in this book have given you many starts. Your task now is to select some of your starts and find ways of pushing them towards a destination that is not yet known. Go back to some of your work and ask yourself: "What happens next? Why? And then what happens? Why?" Carry on until you reach something that feels like an "end." Once you arrive at your destination, ask yourself the big question: Now that I know where I am going, where should I begin?

That does not mean you will begin your story by alluding to or reflecting the end or some sense of change. There are many, many, many ways to begin. (Read other stories and novels analytically to find ways to begin your stories.) It does mean, however, that you will begin your story where your story should begin. Where is that? Only your heart and mind and knowledge of where it is going to end (and a lot of analytical reading) can tell you. Then the work really begins. It becomes your job to make the journey truly worthwhile. For yourself. And the reader.

So if you feel unhappy with how a story begins, and you are spending a lot of time tinkering with the opening, or you are feeling blocked because you are unhappy with the opening, it could be that you have not pushed the story through to its end and therefore have no way of knowing where it should begin. So forge on. Get to the end before you start to work on a new beginning to your story.

And in the end…

Speaking of destinations, how do you end a story? After all, ultimately it is the end that we are leading up to.

First, make sure you have completed at first draft, even if you feel you really haven't discovered where the story is supposed to end, before you do any significant editing. In other words, push it to someplace that feels like it could be the end or at least sort of finished. Then take time off to think.

A story needs a resolution—a climax and denouement. Now a deliberate lack of a resolution can be a resolution, so your story doesn't have to be tied up all neatly in a bow. But you do have to look back and ask yourself: who is/are the central character(s). What is/are the central issue(s). How is it (are they) resolved (or not resolved)?

If you don't have that at the end of your story, close your eyes and visualize it. What is the main issue, the central conflict of the story? How is it (or should it be) resolved (or not resolved)? Who is involved in the resolution? What do they do or say or think or feel (or all of the above) in order to reach that point of resolution (or understanding that there will be no resolution)? Open your eyes and write what you saw….

Once you have that ending down, reflect on it. Again, close your eyes...

Where do you see your protagonist at the very end of all this, after the resolution—maybe minutes or days or weeks or years afterwards? Why? How does she, he or they get there? Is there a path in the story leading beyond the resolution to that place? Where is that place? Why is that place? What is that place: a state of being, of understanding, a physical place, an internal or external place? Visualize it, and then write. Put your protagonist there (with any other significant characters that should be there at the end) and write them into being.

Now all this might feel tacked on. But once you have that ending (climax and denouement), ask yourself if this is where you want the story to end, the place the journey takes you, the reader and your characters. And ask yourself if all that comes before the ending leads you to the end? If not, you have two options:

- Revise the path/journey so it gets you to the ending you want
- Revise the ending so it is somewhere that the story leads to.

Ending exercise

All that is fine in theory, but there is something you can do—beyond thinking and visualizing—to help you discover your story ending. Remember the delta factor exercise in Chapter 4?

In that exercise, you copied your lead—your first paragraph or first several paragraphs—and pasted it on to the end of the story.

When you do this, you have the beginning of your story at the end. Then you ask yourself: What has changed from where this story began? With that in mind, you edit, revise or otherwise hack away at the beginning that you have pasted at the end of your story, and turn it into the ending. It might not look anything like the beginning when you are through with it, and that's okay. All that matters is that you know and understand how and why you got to the end, and that it makes sense to the story.

Then, of course, you go back to the beginning and see if, based on the ending, you should revise where your story starts. The circle is all part of the process of making the story as focused and complete as possible.

19 / Chunking to Create an Outline

The modern novel tends to run about 350 pages with about 350 words per page. That's 122,500 words. Divide that by maybe 15 chapters and you get just over 8,000 words per chapter. (You can have more or fewer words in the novel, more or fewer words per chapter, more or fewer chapters. The main thing is that you tell the story.) Each chapter should tell a section or segment of the story. The reader should be able to shut the novel at the end of a chapter feeling as if they are closing the book on a segment of the life of the main character (protagonist). At the same time, you want to leave the reader wanting to know what happens next. So there should be feelings of suspense as well at the end of each chapter. That is what sustains the reader—the ups and downs that run through the life of the main character leading up to the climax of the book.

In many ways, this might seem like a consciously manipulative way of writing. And it is. But the first draft can spring from freefall, without the author knowing where it is all going to go. Get the story down on paper. Then let your internal editor look at it and make conscious decisions as to how to develop character and plot, build in suspense, and end each chapter leaving the reader curious about what happens next.

So why tell you all of this?

The process I just describe can be rather intimidating. And intimidation can lead to blocks. The intimidation factor can block your writing; however, there is something you can do to alleviate it. It's called chunking. Chunking is the process of breaking a large task down into a series of small steps. First, create a rough outline of the idea, from beginning to end. The outline is not carved in stone; it does not lock you in. It simply lets you mull over how your idea might unfold. You jot down how it might unfold so you have a sense of the big picture: what you are trying to accomplish and how you are going to do it.

As your idea unfolds in writing, you may find yourself following your outline religiously (many genre writers will not start to write until they have first produced a detailed outline, which they follow from point to point to point, chapter to chapter to chapter). Or you may find yourself meandering away from your outline or revising it as you write. I like to revise my outline as I complete each major section or chapter of anything I write; that way, when I sit down to write the next day, I fell I know where to start and where to go. If I stray or meander, no problem. I can always revise my outline at the end of the day. But revising it at the end of each chapter or section helps keep me on track.

And yes, you may find yourself ignoring it all together as you simply continue to explore your idea. What ever works for you is fine. But notice something kind of neat: no matter which scenario your follow, you are writing.

Chose: blank page or outline?

Which would you rather have in front of you before you started to write: a blank page or a detailed outline? I am not talking about freefalling or doing other writing exercises. I am talking about before you start to make your idea real. Presumably, you've explored it with clustering, freefall and character development and other exercises. Now you want to write the sucker. Almost anybody I ask says they'd rather start with an outline on the page, but few writers do. (Why do we insist on making this process as difficult as possible for ourselves?)

The outline breaks your work down into a series of steps, or chunks, that lead from A to B to C ... Suddenly, the intimidation of the blank page has evaporated. You know where you are going and how you are going to get there. Yes, you still have to write the sucker, but you no longer have to hold the beginning, middle and end in your head. It's on the page before you. All you have to do is follow the yellow brick road, or outline.

Again, the outline does not lock you in. It's not carved in stone. It can be revised, as may be required, as you move forward. At the end of each section or chapter is a great time to review and revise your outline. The next day, you sit down fresh. You know where you've been, where you are going and how you are going to get there.

Intimidation factor gone. Your block should be gone, too.

There are a number of books and websites that talk about creating outlines for fiction and nonfiction. Google the concept and see what you can find. And keep this in mind: Creating an outline cannot hurt your writing in any way. It can help you one heck of a lot, though.

If you want to see a big picture outline, take a look at the table of contents of this book. Before I started to write, I had my big picture outline on the page: the working names of each chapter and the concepts I felt I should address. Also, before I started to write, I outlined the points and the exercises I wanted to make in each chapter. Then, as I finished the first draft of each chapter, I reviewed my big picture outlines (and on occasion move a chapter forward or back) and reviewed the detailed outline of the chapters that I'd be working on next (and on occasion removed or added information). The outline helped me get started and it kept me going. It can help you too.

Create deadlines

Deadlines and outlines dovetail quite nicely. Stick with me and you will see why.

I am a freelance writer. I earn my primary living writing news and magazine articles and documents (case studies, media releases, website content) for clients. Since my livelihood is based on me delivering the right words, on time and on budget, I take my deadlines seriously. But what about this book?

I will be self-publishing the book, so I don't have a publisher breath-ing down my neck asking me when I am going to deliver the manuscript. If I never complete it, I will never publish it. It's as simple as that. But I really would like to write it. I've mentioned it to a few people and they want to read it. Plus, once it's out, I will be able to conduct workshops on overcoming writer's block and will be able to sell a few copies at the workshops.

But I don't have a deadline. A lack of a deadline can lead some writer's into serious bouts of procrastination. Some writers call their procrastination writer's block. I won't argue with them, but I will say this: When you don't have a deadline, its way too easy to not write and to come up with reasons for not writing.

I think you know what I'm going to say next ...

If a deadline has not been imposed upon you, **create your own deadline**. Now if I sat down on Monday and said, "I must have a book finished by Friday," I'd be nuts. Instead, I chunk my deadlines.

I set a date by when I want to have the big picture outline created—the 10 to 15 topics that ultimately become my table of contents. Then I set a deadline for outlining each chapter. Then I set a deadline for writing each chapter, followed by a deadline for taking a break (putting the book in a drawer for a few days or a week). I then set a deadline for reading my first draft, and set deadlines for editing each chapter and for having the book copy edited and proofread. And even for formatting the book, getting the cover designed and publishing it.

And yes, I might start on, say, January 1 and say to myself, "I'd like to have my book on overcoming writer's block published by April 1." But then I chunk my big deadline into a series of small ones based on the actions I have to take to go from blank page to published book.

If you are reading this book, chunking my deadlines worked!

Chunk your book. Create a detailed outline. Create a series of deadlines. Remove the intimidation factor. And write.

But first practice and play. Then find your ideas. Explore them. Chose the one or ones you want to tackle. Explore those ideas in greater detail. Pick the one that you will tackle first. Explore it some more. Get to know your idea, theme, setting, narrative voice, plot and characters intimately. Then outline your book. Set deadlines for the work you want to do. And finally, go forth and do it.

Write it, one chunk at a time, one step at a time, one word, sentence paragraph and chapter at a time. Until you are done.

Do keep this last point in mind: As long as you are writing, there is no such thing as writers block. That doesn't mean every word has to be a gem. It means you have to keep on writing to exercise your writing muscles and to get it in shape for the race you want to run, for the writing you want to do. Once you are in shape, you begin the race.

As you are running, keep this in mind: marathon runners feel pain. They sure as hell want to stop, but they don't. They run through the pain. They also pace themselves and drink a lot of water while running the race.

Run. Pace yourself. Take a break now and then. And you will complete the race.

All the best with your writing!

The next chapter has a few bonus exercises that I hope will help you start writing and keep on writing, until you find your own footing and start to work on your project, or convert one, or more, of these exercises into new projects you want to work on.

20 / Bonus Exercises

To help you move forward, there are a series of bonus writing exercises. I hope these additional exercises will inspire you to continue to write.

1. Put on some classical music, something soothing. Not a march. Use headphones if you have them, and freefall with the music. After five or ten minutes, try a change of pace. Rock 'n' Roll. Frank Sinatra. A march. Whatever. If you have a CD player, iPod or MP3 player with random play, write while your player randomly selects music for you. You may find that the change in music has no effect on your freefall. At the same time, you may find each change transports you to different places. Kind of like being lost in a malfunctioning Star Trek transporter and being randomly transported to different worlds. If you like where you go when you play a particular kind of music, stick with it. But don't be afraid to change the type of music too. The whole point is to get you creating... So take a bit of time, spin a few tunes, and write...
2. Describe your thoughts or feelings about religion in a letter that begins: "Dear God (or address it to whomever your deity may be)...."
3. It's Groundhog Day! Will the sun come out on your writing or will you have six more weeks of cold starts? Write about how you feel about writing right now.

4. Have a conversation with a child about anything of interest to that child. Then, recreate your conversation in a scene that includes dialogue and setting.

5. Take your emotional temperature as you read the daily newspaper. Write a response to the story, article, photograph or letter that evokes the most heat, and send a letter to the editor. Freefall your reply, edit it, and then, if so inclined, send it.

6. Do you know someone who is hard to understand or that you just can't "read"? Write a short piece about what you really think goes on in that person's head. Become that person. Write in first person, starting with "I..."

7. Did you have or do you have a best friend that you admired? Write a note to this person and describe what you admire(d) most about him or her.

8. Describe your dream car or dream vacation on paper. Who would be in the car or on the holiday with you? Where would you go? What would you do once you arrived?

9. The smell of your favourite homemade cookie or a certain someone's musky perfume is hard to forget. Write down five memorable smells and the time in your life that you associate with them. Describe the emotion the scent evokes. Now create a scene in which this scent exists. Who is there? What is going on? Push it into fiction. Or cluster the word "scent" or "aroma" and freefall.

10. Valentine's Day! Write a heartfelt love letter to your significant other or an imaginary lover—without using the word "love."

11. Let God (or your deity) reply to your freefall (exercise #1, above).
12. Write a dialogue between yourself today and yourself of 10, 15 or 20 years ago. Or have your present self write a letter to your past self. Have your past self reply. Write at least 10 letters between the two of you.
13. Are you always satisfied with the fortunes you receive from fortune cookies? Write your own fortune. When that is done, write a story about a fictional person who receives this fortune, and what impact it has on that person when it comes true.
14. Revel in the atmosphere of the season by looking out of a window for a few minutes. Expand on what you see and how it makes you feel, in a brief reflective essay or short fiction piece. Then take two characters that have come out of previous work and put them outside your window, in the scene. Answer in your head: What is their relationship? Why are they there? What are they talking about? Where have they come from? Where are they going? Then write...
15. What is your favourite recipe or dish? Can you cook, or are you horrible at it? Write about cooking.
16. Write an epitaph or obituary, perhaps your own.
17. Write a fictional epitaph or obituary. Then give the person a name, gender, age, date of birth, date of death, birthplace. Where was the person when he or she died? How did he or she die? Who is attending the funeral? Who is not there (who one might think should be there)?
18. Write a story that starts with the above epitaph or obituary. After writing down the epitaph or obituary, flashback to the beginning of the character's life and

outline in point form the significant details of that person's life from start to finish. Freefall from point to point-to-point until you reach the end—and the epitaph or obituary, the reason for those particular words, comes clearly into focus.

19. Take some time off. Seriously. Take some time to walk or to do something completely different. Take an hour or two or a day or two. Walk away from it all, recharge your batteries and then come back refreshed and ready to try something new or work on something old. But do walk away from it once in a while, for at least a little while.

And don't forget...

Freefall daily. Cluster on a regular basis. Plant many seeds. Cultivate the ones that feel like they deserve or require your attention. May many stories bloom!

All the best with your writing!

If you are interested in some personal writing coaching or in taking an online writing course with Paul Lima, please visit www.paullima.com/ecourses or email info@paullima.com.

About the Author

I was seven years old when I published my first magazine. Using a stubby pencil, I meticulously printed articles about members of my family and illustrated the articles with crayon art. I produced only one copy of the magazine, but my entire family read "The Lima News."

I had great fun doing it and words have been an important part of my life ever since...

That's a lovely story, isn't it? However, when I want to sell myself as a writer, I strike a different tone. Just as you have to strike a different tone when you are writing different genres for different audiences. So here's my business tone.

Based in Toronto, Ontario, Paul Lima (www.paullima.com) has worked as a professional writer and business-writing instructor for over 30 years. He has run a successful freelance writing, copywriting, business writing, and media relations training business since 1988. He also coaches writers on the business of freelance writing, writing fiction and articles and self-publishing.

Paul has had short stories and poetry published in numerous literary magazines and online journals and read on CBC Radio. You can read excerpts from some of his short stories at www.paullima.com/cw.

An English major from York University, Paul has worked as a copywriter, continuing education manager and magazine editor.

Additional books by Paul Lima

Paul is the author of a number of books on writing and the business of freelance writing, including the following:

- *Fundamentals of Writing: How to Write Articles, Media Releases, Case Studies, Blog Posts and Social Media Content*
- *How To Write A Non-Fiction Book in 60 Days*
- *Produce, Price and Promote Your Self-Published Fiction or Non-fiction Book and eBook*
- *Everything You Wanted to Know About Freelance Writing - Find, Price, Manage Corporate Writing Assignments & Develop Article Ideas and Sell Them to Newspapers and Magazines*
- *The Six-Figure Freelancer: How to Find, Price and Manage Corporate Writing Assignments*
- *Business of Freelance Writing: How to Develop Article Ideas and Sell Them to Newspapers and Magazines*
- *Harness the Business Writing Process: E-mail, Letters, Proposals, Reports, Media Releases, Web Content*
- *Harness the Email Writing Process: How to Become a More Effective and Efficient Email Writer*
- *How to Write Web Copy and Social Media Content: Spruce up Your Website Copy, Blog Posts and Social Media Content*
- *Say it Right: How to Write Speeches and Presentations*
- *Copywriting That Works: Bright ideas to Help You Inform, Persuade, Motivate and Sell!*
- *How to Write Media Releases to Promote Your Business, Organization or Event*
- *Unblock Writer's Block: How to face it, deal with it and overcome it*
- *(re)Discover the Joy of Creative Writing.*
- *Rebel in the Back Seat and other short stories.*

- *Are You Ready For Your Interview? How to Prepare for Media Interviews How To Write A Non-Fiction Book in 60 Days*

All of the above books are available online in print and/or digital format, from www.paullima.com/books.

All books and short reports are available online in print and/or digital format from www.paullima.com/books.

29280738R00077

Made in the USA
Middletown, DE
21 December 2018